HR Metrics, the World-Class Way

How to enhance your status and build the business case for HR

by Dr. John Sullivan

KENNEDY INFORMATION
Peterborough, NH

ISBN 1-932079-01-7
Copyright ©Kennedy Information
All rights reserved.

Published by Kennedy Information, Inc.
Peterborough, New Hampshire
Publishers of *The Directory of Executive Recruiters,*
The Directory of Outplacement and Career Management Firms,
Search Select®, Executive Recruiter News, and *Recruiting Trends.*

Kennedy Information
One Phoenix Mill Lane
5th Floor
Peterborough, NH 03458
603-924-1006
bookstore@kennedyinfo.com
www.KennedyInfo.com

About the Author

Dr. John Sullivan is a well-known HR "guru," international speaker, author, and advisor to *Fortune* 500 and global 1000 firms. Over the course of his career, Dr. Sullivan has continuously challenged the HR profession, driving individuals and corporations to "world-class" performance. Dr. Sullivan's efforts focus on "Changing the DNA" of the HR profession to create a function capable of building and sustaining competitive advantage through talent. His ability to "push the envelope" of HR has led many industry publications to name Dr. Sullivan one of the most influential people in the field of HR. Distinctions earned include being named one of *PersonnelToday's* "40 Power Players," and *Recruiter Magazine's* "Top 100 Most Influential People in the Recruiting Industry."

Training Magazine has called him a "visionary" and named him as one of its top thought leaders. *Fast Company* magazine called him "the Michael Jordan of hiring"! Industry guru Gerry Crispin called him "the "Tom Peters of HR" because of his energetic presentation style. Tom Peters called his e-HR work "brilliant."

Dr. Sullivan is a founding contributor to the Electronic Recruiting Exchange, where he publishes a weekly column on the preeminent issues facing the recruiting profession. His thoughts and opinions can also be found via articles appearing in the *IHRIM Journal, Workforce* Magazine, Monster.com, and the *VP-of-HR* Newsletter, of which he is the editor.

Background:

Dr. Sullivan served in the corporate world as the Chief Talent Officer for Agilent Technologies, the 43,000-employee spin-off of Hewlett-Packard, where he managed US recruiting, workforce planning, and retention strategy. He currently serves as a Professor and Head of the Human Resource Management Program at San Francisco State University. Prior to accepting roles with Agilent Technologies and San Francisco State University, Dr. Sullivan held roles as the CEO of a start-up organization, Director of

Training, Research Manager, and Executive Director. He is the founder of the California Strategic Human Resources Partnership, a consortium of 33 leading HR Vice Presidents from *Fortune* 500 firms located in California.

Dr. Sullivan holds Ph.D., M.B.A., and B.Sc. degrees in Human Resource Management from the University of Florida.

Also by Dr. John Sullivan

Improving Productivity, the World-Class Way:
A Simple but Effective Productivity Toolkit for Managers
World-class managers manage with performance in mind. In this ground-breaking new book, Dr. John Sullivan discusses building an organizational culture around performance, and provides you with an arsenal of tools that have helped leading organizations advance by leaps and bounds over their competition. Readers can expect to learn about such topics as energizing your employees, assessing your workforce, retaining key talent, and metrics for measuring personal productivity.

Recruiting by Line Managers, the World-Class Way:
A Strategy Toolkit for Creating and Keeping Competitive Advantage in HR
Written for line managers looking for big recruiting results with just a little investment of time, the managers' recruiting toolkit presents a series of 65 tools proven to be effective by leading companies. Tools cover everything from finding top-caliber talent to getting them to accept an offer. This book captures all of the top tools in use by many of America's most respected names in business.

Corporate Recruiting, the World-Class Way:
A Powerful Toolkit for Recruiting and Retaining the Best of the Best
It has been said numerous times that talent is the last avenue for developing competitive advantage in the global economy. More than ever before, firms must focus on strategically managing the tools and infrastructure that bring talent into the organization and on attempting to retain it. In this comprehensive book, Dr. Sullivan introduces the tools and strategies behind world-class recruiting at the corporate level. No organization should be without this toolkit. When recruiting challenges arise, simply sort through any number of innovative tools to generate leads of top candidates capable of adding value to your organization. Use chapters on strategy to develop your own differentiated talent strategy, validate your objectives, and identify applicable metrics to measure your effectiveness.

VP-of-HR Newsletter™

The *VP-of-HR* Newsletter is the strategic newsletter for senior HR executives of *Fortune* 500 firms and those aspiring to the role. The goal of *VP-of-HR* is to offer out-of-the-box solutions and alternatives to the traditional ways of approaching HR. Approximately half of the articles are "think pieces" whose primary purpose is to cause you to step back and take a second look at traditional HR practices. Many of the remaining articles discuss more practical tools and strategies that are designed to give you answers to current and emerging issues in human resources. The assumption from the beginning is that you already know how "most people do it," so the newsletter won't waste your time with traditional solutions. Free subscriptions are available at www.drjohnsullivan.com.

ER Daily Column, ERExchange.com

Published by the Electronic Recruiting Exchange every weekday, the ER Daily Newsletter provides insight into the latest in recruiting tools, hiring strategies, and trends in the recruiting industry. Subscribers can look forward to articles by Dr. Sullivan every Monday on topics ranging from strategic workforce planning to employment branding. Into addition to cutting-edge articles, subscribers can respond directly to the author, or strike up on on-line debate with fellow subscribers. Subscriptions are available for free at www.erexchange.com.

IHRIM Column, *IHRIM Journal*

The *IHRIM Journal* is a quarterly publication by the International Association for Human Resource Information Management (IHRIM). The *IHRIM Journal*'s content is specifically written for executive management and senior-level Human Resource and Information Technology leadership (e.g., CEOs, CIOs, VPs, and Directors), university professors and students, and other current or emerging thought leaders and visionaries. Readers can turn to Dr. Sullivan's column in every issue to read about his views on the latest controversial issues facing the human resource profession. More information about the *IHRIM Journal* can be found out www.ihrim.org.

Acknowledgments

Writing is an activity that some people enjoy, and that others despise. I happen to be one of those people who enjoy it. I have spent well over 30 years in the field of HR, and each has brought with it new learning and new challenges. Solving complex business problems and continuously pushing the envelope of world-class performance in HR is my passion, and I am thankful that so many people have found value in my observations and perspectives on emerging issues.

Throughout my professional career, many individuals have shared in my passion, and in some way or another contributed to the book you hold today. Some of my former students have challenged me, forcing me to test my own views, while professionals have enlightened me, and shared with me the best practices that have set them and their firms apart.

It would be very difficult to give proper credit to all of the people who have helped me in one way or another to finish this book. If I were to list all who have played a role in developing who I am, then it is safe to say that the list would fill yet another book. However, I would like to take this opportunity to thank two people who played a tremendous role in helping to select material for, assemble, and polish this book. Over the past several years two former students, Susan Wong and Master Burnett, have helped elevate my work to another level. They have made my lists more precise and my views more clear, and have helped to fill in any gaps that might have existed in my logic.

I also need to thank all of the people at Kennedy Information who have worked so hard to make this book and the "World-class Way" series of books a reality. Putting together a book is much harder than you might think, and requires a great deal of time. Many thanks to Wayne Cooper, R.D. Whitney, and Jack Burnett for being so patient with me as I revised and added to the first draft. Jack invested many hours in making sure that my writing style would not pain those of you who can spot a grammatical violation from a mile away, and his efforts are greatly appreciated.

To everyone who has assisted me over the years or contributed to my development, I wish to express my thanks.

Table of Contents

Chapter Three: Training Metrics 93

Chapter Four: Compensation Metrics .109

HR Metrics, the World-Class Way

How to enhance your status and build the business case for HR

by Dr. John Sullivan

Introduction

The goal of this book

The primary purpose of this book is to excite you about the use of metrics in HR. Admittedly that has often been a daunting task, since most articles and books on the subject tend to be a little on the dry side. In contrast, the format of this book is designed so that if you don't have time to read it all the way through, you can go directly to the topics that interest you and use it as a toolkit or reference source. Feel free to skip between chapters and the sections, depending on your interest and the problems you're facing.

Note that if a set of metrics you are considering seems at first to be complicated, don't be alarmed. The most effective metrics are simple, and they use easily available information. Here's why: (1) No HR manager wants to become a statistics expert and (2) most of them find that merely using metrics (no matter how simple they are) as the basis for their arguments gains them 75 percent of the credibility they need. Adding additional or complex metrics has some but not a major impact on their success rate.

So fear not. Using metrics can be easy and impactful.

The "New HR" and the important role metrics play

Goal of this chapter

Before you embark on the process of developing metrics, it's important to realize that the business world is changing rapidly. Because of those changes,

HR as a function must change equally as fast. This chapter highlights the changing role of HR, which I call "the new HR." You'll find that the "new HR" requires a more aggressive and businesslike approach to solving "people problems" then most HR professionals are accustomed to. Once you understand the new expectations, you will then see why you can't survive in the new world of HR without including metrics in everything you do.

HR's Changing Role

Times change, people adapt, and the way we do business evolves. From influences relating to the introduction of technology, to new emerging global economies, the factors that spur change are numerous. Within the modern business enterprise, few functions work the same way they did 30 years ago, and HR is no exception.

Today, while still responsible for many operational roles, HR is growing more strategic — although the transformation is taking longer than many would like. So what should we do to resolve this predicament?

The Next Step — Becoming an HR Leader

An HR leader forecasts business needs and, using HR tools, increases the organization's capacity to beat the competition. In short, an HR leader has a measurable business impact. The key operational word here is measurable. An HR leader goes beyond the traditional role of "business partner," who generally only reacts to requests. Rather, an HR leader is someone who anticipates business opportunities and problems and suggests action prior to being asked by management. An HR leader directly impacts

- The business,

- Its products, and

- Its profitability.

An HR leader ensures that every dollar spent on HR/People services has a higher rate of return than similar investments in plant and equipment. An HR leader is a business leader who happens to work in the HR department!

"Business partner" is a term that was invented by HR people for HR people. It's OK to use it "among friends"; however, I know several senior vice presidents of HR who react harshly to the term. It implies that we are seeking to be an equal partner, when in reality we must earn respect by actions, not just words. CEOs find it strange in many cases because other staff functions don't use it. When playing with the "big boys and girls," use their language, which is "business *leader*"!

To further stir the pot, let me say that I find that most of the people I know who use even this business partner term are simply "wanna-be's." Real leadership is obvious: It has a measurable impact on profitability, and it doesn't need a word to describe it.

Becoming a Leader Means Thinking Like One

HR professionals are traditionally different than other business professionals: They act differently, speak a different language, and definitely make decisions differently. While the rest of the organization focuses on revenue and profit growth and increasing a firm's capabilities and capacities, most of HR focuses on issues within the enterprise that contribute little and cost a lot, such as benefits administration.

Most human resource systems and processes were developed in the first half of the 20th century to meet the business needs at that time, but the times have changed and most of our HR systems and processes have not. The new constant for business is faster, more customer-focused, of higher quality and lower cost. Markets and products now change so rapidly that the window of opportunity for the profitability of a new product can sometimes be measured in weeks rather than years. The life of a major company used to be measured in decades while in the current world major company's can go from greatness to failure in a matter of months. Firms like Enron, Global Crossing, Arthur Andersen, and WorldCom are but a few examples of how fast and how hard mismanaged companies can fall.

Human resources have continually failed to adapt to this changing pattern, and as a result it is at risk of being left behind. The code word for success in the next decade and beyond will be *agility* (the ability to move resources rapidly toward high-impact business areas, where rapidness is measured in hours, days, and weeks).

The premise is clear: In order to react to the quantum pace of change, we must be able to

1. Rapidly move resources away from low-return areas to the areas of high business opportunity or

2. More accurately predict the future so that we can be prepared for it.

The latter, although a desirable goal, has been proven to be difficult to reach. So the most reasonable option is to develop systems that are designed to rapidly react to a predictable range of business options. For example, few can successfully predict when the stock market will rise or fall, but if you presume that both will happen periodically, you can develop management systems to take advantage of movement in either direction. In other cases, such as computer chips and disk drives, the range of possibilities is one-dimensional — they will get only faster and cheaper, with more features. Thus you have to be prepared only for *when* a certain speed, capability, and cost will be obtained.

Killing HR History: Agility Is the Future

In order for HR to make a quantum step in its evolution and to be successful, our systems and processes must be changed radically to meet the needs of the changing market. To accomplish this, HR must transform itself away from being an operational or overhead organization and assume a leadership role. We must follow the lead of other business units like finance, manufacturing, marketing, and supply chain by relying heavily on the use of metrics to identify where resources can best be allocated within the firm to maximize competitive position. In short, HR must become a master at using metrics to drive the organization.

Steps in developing an agile HR function

To develop this new, more agile organization, HR *must:*

1. Identify what resources can be shifted toward a business opportunity. Resources available to HR usually include:

    *   Cash or budget allocation
    *   People or head count allocation
    *   Management assistance (training, management time, and people management effective tools)
    *   Historical/current information (performance data and best practices) necessary for decision-making
    *   New strategies, approaches or processes

2. Drop the concept of equal and consistent treatment as a goal. Organizations can't do everything well and if they try, they actually hurt themselves. The new goal for HR is to put an unequal share of the resources into areas of high opportunity (return) and divert them, either permanently or temporarily, from low-return areas. Just like in competitive sports, not everyone can get equal playing time or management support.

3. Identify barriers to the rapid movement of resources, and
    minimize or eliminate as many as possible. Some typical barriers
    might include:

    *   A culture that rejects everything that was "not invented here"
        or that delays new approaches that everyone doesn't agree with
    *   Yearlong budgets without a contingency reallocation process
    *   Approval processes that involve multi-levels of management
    *   Fixed compensation and benefit systems
    *   Non-project-based time allocation systems
    *   Fixed head count controls
    *   Individuals who protect their own "silos" and territory

4. Identify the possible range of change or shifts that the market will
    require. The possible shift that will be required may be as small as
    a 5% shift in retail foodstuffs, to a 20% shift in the financial
    markets, to as much as a 33% shift in certain high-tech areas. By
    studying your competitors and market trends, the range of
    possible shifts can, in fact, be predicted relatively accurately.

5. Recruit management support. Your management "champions"
    (historical supporters of improved people practices) need to
    change the mind-set of others away from a philosophy that
    marginal change is enough, toward an approach of continually
    rethinking systems and processes where speed and responsiveness
    to market forces are needed. Once the mind-set is changed, you
    will find that some individuals and teams are "agile" and others
    are not. Agility can be taught, but sometimes it's best to focus on
    those who "can" and reassign those who can't think differently to
    other low impact areas.

In conclusion: I have found that HR is often the last to "get it." Most HR
organizations hang on to HR processes and programs long past their use-
fulness. Many HR organizations also allow different functions to operate

independently within "functional silos." We in HR have some control over huge resources (if you count total compensation and benefits, HR often controls over 60% of a company's operational budget), but speed or agility in moving in these resources has seldom been an HR goal. With the reality of the "new market forces," speed and agility can in fact be the ticket to finally making HR a "business leader" and "the" driver of business change. Now is the time to seize the opportunity!

Now that you see HR's changing role, the next step is understanding why metrics are so necessary and what a good metric looks like.

Chapter One

Metrics, an Introduction

Goal of this chapter

After over 30 years of studying HR departments I have found that the largest single difference between a great HR department and an average one, is the extensive use of metrics.

After metrics, the second most important factor is a large differential in rewards, based primarily on performance. Bar none, there is nothing you can do to improve yours and your department's performance that exceeds the impact of using metrics. More training, more budget, better pay, or even more head count will not have the same impact as utilizing metrics. But before you can utilize metrics you have to understand that.

The goal of this chapter is to demystify metrics, to show you their benefits and what differentiates a good metric from a great one. When the term "metrics" comes up in an HR conversation, the look on people's faces ranges from one of complete happiness to one of complete horror. The range in reactions primarily has to do with the audience privy to the conversation. For those new to collecting data and preparing metrics, the reaction is often horror. In contrast, for those experienced in using metrics, the reaction is more positive because they know that it dramatically increases their chance of getting a project approved by senior management, who live and die "by the numbers." It turns out that metrics are similar to the introduction of technology. Initially there is a fear when you start to use them, but eventually they become an indispensable way of life.

Why the thought of having to prepare metrics evokes such fear for some people is no mystery. Most previous approaches to the subject make it seem like rocket science, but rest easy: Metrics are not as complicated as many would have you believe! They generally don't have to be complicated or sophisticated in order to have an impact.

What follows is a quick introduction to metrics. This section explains what makes a metric a metric, some of the benefits that can be realized from using them, and some of the HR strategies that rely on them.

The motto going forward is: *Without numbers, it's just an opinion!*

Metrics by themselves have little value unless they are put into use on a regular basis. This is a common problem with many measurement efforts. Data is often collected, but little or — in many cases — nothing is done with it.

To make the use of metrics more widespread in HR, consider using some of the many HR metric tools outlined in this book in your next project.

What Makes a Metric a Metric?

In short, a metric is simply using a number to enhance a story or argument. A metric is never "just a word." Instead, it is a number that when he added to words makes an argument more powerful. Unfortunately, many HR people describe their results using words alone. And while using words exclusively to describe a result might make an interesting argument, adding metrics or numbers to quantify the result is what makes the story truly powerful.

- ✓ A word — We were successful.

- ✓ A metric — We met our target of processing 20 relocations.

- ✓ A better metric — We met our target of processing 20 new relocations, with a zero error rate and a 100 percent customer satisfaction rate.

Why metrics are superior to "numbers" — telling a more complete story
Metrics are generally used to measure results or output. The difference between a metric and a number is that a metric normally has several elements or parts.

An example —

- ✓ A manager can say that he or she successfully completed 20 units. That would be a number (20 units).

A performance metric, in contrast, goes deeper into describing the result. It tells a more complete five-part story.

1. Quantity — I completed 20 units

2. Quality — of the 20 units, 10 percent had defects

3. Time — the 20 units were due by October 1st, but they weren't completed until October 15th

4. Cost or money — the target cost for the 20 units was $1,000; the actual cost was $2,000

5. Customer service/satisfaction — the normal return rate from customers is 1 out of 20 units. The return rate for this production run was 10 out of 20.

Most people would be satisfied with the first "number" (20 units produced), but after looking at the more complete performance metric, most would judge the production run to be a complete failure.

Don't forget to also include a measure of quality

Metrics, like most things, come in a range of effectiveness. The best metrics tell a "complete" story. Those metrics that tell a more thorough, complete, and powerful story include not just the "number" of occurrences but also add to that number a measure of quality. For example, stating that you "won three Olympic medals" does not tell the same story as "I won three gold medals." Great metrics include both the basic number and an indication of quality (where quality means value, rank, or impact).

Here's another example. Let's use a metric that is often reported in HR, the number of new hires per period of time (we hired five engineers last month). As a number, this metric does tell a story: It tells us that during a particular specified period of time, we successfully hired a specific number of candidates.

For the highly interested manager, though, this metric doesn't tell a complete story. In its present form, it defines merely a single characteristic of our hiring efforts, numerical success. However, by combining two or more characteristics together, we build a more complete story.

In this case, if we add a measure of quality to the number-of-hires metric we end up with a metric that tells managers a more complete story (we hired five engineers last month and 100 percent of them exceeded the job requirements). This metric, when compared to the initial "number of hires" metric, is a clear indicator of whether our hiring efforts have been successful (assuming that we have defined in advance what percentage of hires should exceed the job requirements). It takes a little more work, but adding the quality aspect makes it a more powerful "story."

This simple exercise demonstrates that the more complete the story our metrics tell, the more empowered we are to make decisions — decisions that are now powered by fact, not emotion. That's what qualitative metrics do. They help us to improve our arguments to management, to accomplish more, and ultimately to continually to improve so that we can beat the competition. In short, metrics and numbers are the language of business, and failing to utilize metrics is the primary thing that has kept HR out of the "big leagues" and under the CFO's budget-cutting scrutiny for years.

Benefits of Doing Metrics

The benefits of doing metrics are numerous, but let's walk through them quickly, to make sure that you are aware of each of them.

The most difficult aspect of HR isn't designing good programs or processes — that's the easy part. The challenge is actually changing the way managers and employees act (the technical term is changing "behavior"). Unfortunately, facts, data, and information don't automatically change behavior. But they do have a major impact on most people and they have the largest impact on people who are logical and systematic. Fortunately, most senior managers, engineers, and finance, marketing, and technical people are logical and systematic. And that's why in many cases they demand metrics or they won't even listen.

That's where metrics come in. In business, most decisions are made on an economic basis according to "the numbers." Budgeting, market research, and technology all rely on metrics. That is why managers and employees often make "people issues" a low priority — because they involve feelings and behaviors, which HR often fails to quantify. For example, when a "people-related" behavior is harming the organization in some way but the effects are not readily apparent, getting the people involved to change is difficult, because others see your request not as a fact but instead as a difference of opinion. In contrast, when you wrap your solution in metrics that quantify the damage using actual data that demonstrates the severity of the issue, your request is immediately differentiated from an opinion. Why, because true experts use data and metrics, rather than opinions, because they carry a much stronger weight. In a similar light, opportunities are viewed more positively when they are supported with data and metrics.

Eliminate confusion about what's important. Using metrics can also eliminate any confusion in the organization as to what is truly valued. As a consultant, I cannot count how many times I have walked into a corporate headquarters and seen the values of the organization painted on the wall, only to then see policies and rewards that incent actions in direct opposition to those stated values (Enron serves as an excellent example of this problem). Stating that something is important, but then failing to measure to what degree you have achieved success with regard to those statements, is a very visible indication that what is stated as important truly isn't valued.

"What you measure (and reward) sends the clearest possible message to your employees about what is important … and what isn't."

Determine what to reward. If metrics tell people what is important, rewards get them to do it faster! Metrics can be used to indicate clearly what actions exceed average performance, and therefore warrant some positive reaction from management such as praise or a reward. For years, this is one benefit that HR has underused, often providing benefits (rewards) to employees on an equal basis and thereby sending a negative message to top performers that management feels that all employees contribute equally.

Focus. Metrics also play a critical role in identifying where HR resources need to be focused. Because you can't do it all well, it is important to send a clear message to your HR employees about what is important and what is less important.

Such areas where focus is needed could include problems that are limiting the success of the organization, or opportunities that could provide the firm an enhanced competitive advantage. Agile organizations and leading CEOs excel at prioritizing and focusing at the organizational level, and expectations are rising for HR to become expert at focusing their resources as well. Identifying what factors have the most impact on success and failure within an organization, and then continuously monitoring those factors using metrics, enables HR to become more proactive versus reactive in allocating resources under its control.

Continuous improvement. It's not good enough to fix a problem or to be the best. In a fast-changing world, you must constantly improve. There is no standing still. By comparing "today's" performance to "yesterday's" over time, you track the rate that you continually improve. In many HR departments it's important to improve what you do in HR at least as fast as the rate of improvement of your product. Continuous improvement is something that can be achieved only through the use of metrics. By definition, continuous improvement is something that you need to do on a continuous basis. Diagnostic metrics can be tied to each of the major milestones of a process in order to help identify what stages of the activity can be improved.

Self-confidence. HR professionals are no different than other employees. They want to know how well they are doing in their job. Measuring results through metrics allows individuals to self-assess how well they are doing without having to wait for one senior performance appraisal. Knowing how well you are doing can build your confidence and give you the courage to try new approaches.

Demonstrate a results-oriented mentality. This last benefit — but by all means not so in importance — is that using metrics demonstrates to all managers (and shareholders) that you too are focused on results. Demonstrating that you are results-oriented increases your credibility among such stakeholders, and helps ensure that when their assistance or loyalty is needed, it will be available.

The Consequences of Not Using Metrics

Not using metrics comes with a host of negative consequences, most of which you can easily discern from looking at the opposites of the advantages. Failing to use metrics may also mean a cut in your budget, fewer opportunities for new projects, and a slower-moving career. In short, not using metrics may demonstrate:

- That you are part of the "old school" of HR, which regards measurement as unimportant;

- That actual output or results are not important to you in making decisions;

- That becoming a top performer and achieving status as "the best" is not your desire;

- That you are not interested in what economic return you are getting for the corporate dollars you have invested; and

- That excellence and continuous improvement are not valued.

In many organizations (especially those in finance, technology, and any organization that uses Six Sigma), failure to utilize metrics can be a career-limiting or -ending choice. In the "new HR," metrics are an essential part of life!

The Ultimate Driver for Metrics: Changing Behaviors

As noted in the last section, using metrics as a tool to change behavior is one of the benefits of using metrics. Changing behavior is something with which many organizations struggle. As humans, most of us have a desire to avoid conflict, and experience has demonstrated that asking someone to change the way they do something often results in conflict. Fortunately, the use of metrics has proven to be a powerful tool in changing behavior because it steers any potential conflict away from opinions and personalities and toward facts. Metrics can be used to change behaviors that have proven unchangeable by using traditional change tactics including:

- Asking ("please")

- Nonmonetary rewards ("thank you")

- Information and communication efforts (newsletters)

- Vision/values statements

- Training

Facts and metrics that are applied across the entire organization make most arguments less emotional because everyone is being measured using the same criteria. Because everyone must change and make their numbers, requests for change seem less personal.

An example; TV and magazines run hundreds of ads asking people not to speed. But placing a police car with a precisely accurate radar (metrics) not only instantly reduces speeding but it also reduces court appearances in which the driver "feels the need" to argue their case.

The basic steps
Before you use metrics to change behavior, you first have to identify what you want an individual or department to do "more of or less of." Be specific. Having identified what specific actions need to be reduced and which need to increase, the next step is to develop metrics that measure

the degree to which your expectations are being met. Next, identify the current performance level for each goal and compare it to the expected standard. Discuss the differential in the proposed standards with those involved to ensure that the standards and expectations are reasonable. With your metrics in mind, set a schedule or timetable of expectations and make sure that it is realistic. When the results are improving, reward those involved using rewards they value, and withhold rewards when metrics (results) worsen.

The Value of "Distributing" Metrics in Order to Change Behavior

The most common error in the use of metrics is also the one with the largest negative impact. The error is keeping results metrics confidential or available only to a limited few. In stark contrast to that, I recommend distributing "ranked" performance metrics throughout the organization. Post them on the walls and in the corporate intranet site. It's important to share metrics with those involved because keeping them a secret might lead to confusion about what is expected. Also, confidentiality helps only to avoid "public comparisons" with others and will only delay the results you will achieve. If relevant metrics are distributed to all managers on a regular basis, they have the impact of:

- Embarrassing the poor performers

- Recognizing or highlighting the top performers

- Energize those who thought they were doing "OK"

- Taking away "ignorance" as an excuse for poor performance ("I thought everyone was in the same boat as me")

- Showing the weak who is good, so that they can learn directly from them

- Showing all what the benchmark top performance level is, so that they can raise their expectations

- Showing everyone that management is serious about performance

If you also include in the distributed metrics the best-in-class "results" from competitors and the best-performing firms in your industry, you might also energize people's competitive juices toward becoming the best in the industry.

An additional performance tip: If the tools that the best (and worst performers) utilize are listed in the report alongside their results, others can also know which tools "work" (and don't work) within your culture.

Results should be listed by name, and they should be ranked from best to worst so that everyone knows at a glance where they stand.

Metrics Are Easy: The Five Main Types of Metrics (QQTM & CS)

I have said it time and time again: Metrics are easy. However, getting to the point where conceiving and using metrics is second nature requires a little change in the way we describe results. Traditionally, HR has used what others in business would consider soft metrics — things like employee satisfaction and compass. In contrast, the rest of the enterprise utilized hard metrics including things like unit output, error rates, and return on investment (ROI). The two approaches are radically different, and although each has its place in the agile organization, HR must learn to increase its use of the underutilized hard metrics — for it is these that measure performance in terms that other executives, including the CEO and CFO, use every day in their decision-making.

Hard metrics: The first four elements listed below are sometimes classified as hard metrics. They are the metrics that are used primarily by financial and technology professionals. They are called hard metrics because they generally measure "visible" or tangible things. Hard metrics generally fall into one of four categories (quality, quantity, time and money), while the fifth metric element (customer satisfaction) is sometimes called a "soft" metric.

The five elements of a complete metric
Within HR there are five basic elements to any metrics or measure of results. Generally, each of the five elements (although there are some exceptions) are needed in order to make a "complete" metric.

Quality. Measures the error rate or the quality of the output of a process. For example, HR can measure the "quality" of a particular recruiting source by looking at the on-the-job performance of the hires that each source produced. Quality recruiting sources produce more top-performing employees than average recruiting sources.

Quantity. Measures the numerical output of a given process over a specified period of time. For example, a training professional might use a quantity metric to report the average number of formal training hours delivered to a particular individual/population over the course of a year. Quantity metrics generally mean just "counting the number" produced.

Time. Measures the speed or elapsed period of time with which a specified action or process is completed from start to finish. A common example found within HR is time-to-fill, which represents the elapsed time between the moment a requisition for a new hire is introduced and a suitable candidate is hired.

Money. Measures the cost or revenues associated with or produced by a specified action or process. Within HR, cost metrics are fairly common; however, few organizations have attempted to measure the revenue associated with particular HR efforts. A common example of a cost metric used in HR is cost per hire.

Customer satisfaction. Measures the degree to which the outcome of the process matches the expectations as defined by the customer of the action or process. Within HR, customer satisfaction metrics can be used to identify to what degree candidates from staffing meet the hiring manager's expectations, and how interviewed candidates view our selection process. Customer satisfaction is sometimes classified as a "soft measure" because it is measuring feelings or other intangible things.

World-Class HR Metrics —
a Checklist for Assessing Where You Stand

Use this simple list as a measuring stick for assessing your first set of metrics and then utilize it to improve your metrics over time. When you can say that all eighteen characteristics apply to your metrics, you are truly world-class.

- ✓ They are based on (or relate to) numbers and ratios that are readily available in the company's annual report, 10K, or 10Q.

- ✓ They use the ratios, formulas, and language already used by the CFO in other company strategic reports/metrics — not HR jargon.

- ✓ They focus on the quality of the results and outputs rather than just on costs. All major metrics include quality as well as cost elements.

- ✓ When possible, they directly relate to business issues (profit, customer satisfaction, sales) rather than just HR issues.

- ✓ Where possible, they don't just report results — they also they show cause and effect.

- ✓ Metrics that are ineffective or that demonstrate a low added value to decision-making are periodically dropped from use.

- ✓ They have face validity (they are viewed as believable by non-experts).

- ✓ They are distributed widely internally and ranked in order of value, often with side-by-side comparisons of current performance to past performance.

- ✓ They are designed to mesh with and to be consistent with budgeting and other corporate measurement/resource allocation systems.

✓ They include customer service/responsiveness components.

✓ They allow for external comparisons against best-in-class firms.

✓ They are hard to "manipulate," and the method used to collect the data is consistent and reasonable.

✓ The data is collected in the most economical way possible (e.g., random sampling is used whenever possible).

✓ When possible, data is reported in performance-level segments (or quartiles) so that top performers can be segregated from bottom performers.

✓ They include ROI (return on investment) calculations whenever possible.

✓ Those being measured are involved in the process.

✓ A metric, when used as an indicator of individual performance, actually measures output from processes and programs that the individual owns or has some control over (it's unfair to measure someone on something over which they have no input or control).

✓ When used, they actually change behavior so that low scores on individual and departmental metrics continually improve over time.

Common Problems with HR Metrics

Once people get excited about using metrics, the tendency is to go way overboard and attempt to measure everything. Unfortunately, going overboard is not the only common problem found among professionals that use metrics in HR. Outlined below are a few of the major problems I have encountered during my many years of consulting. Keep these potential problems in mind as you go forward.

Too many metrics! The goal of using metrics is to help improve performance in an organization. It would be nice if we could measure everything, but the truth is that we have limited resources and time. When starting out, you may need to run (use) more metrics to determine which ones provide value and which do not. However, over time the number of metrics in use should be pared down to the smallest set possible. While there is no absolute rule that tells us "the right number" of metrics to use, I would recommend that no single individual be responsible for maintaining more than from four to ten different metrics (unless collecting data and preparing metrics is the individual's sole function).

Focusing on effort, not output. Numerous metrics in use today exemplify this common error. Measuring effort is relatively easy. It is often as simple as calculating the time spent providing some good or service. But simply providing the time side of the story does not tell us the actual impact of the effort. Not all efforts produce results. Metrics should measure the resulting outcome from a particular action or process. For example, many training metrics focus on the number of hours provided to each employee, but few go to the next level and identify what impact each training hour had on employee productivity.

Focusing on quantity, not quality. Just as in making the "effort, not output" error that was cited in the last item, many HR metrics measure only the quantitative output, without looking at its quality. One common example is found in the staffing function, when we look at the volume of applications produced by a particular source such as an employment ad, employee referral program, and or similar. Rarely do firms look beyond the volume and determine what percentage of the candidates exceeds a preselected quality standard. In order to tell the complete story, the staffing function needs to track and identify both the quantity and the quality of applicants.

Failing to establish a comparison. A single metric collected from a single point in time can be useful only if you have some standard with which to compare it. Great metrics provide comparison numbers (such as this year to last, compared to our goals, compared to the best in the industry, or compared to the best in the world) so that you can measure improvement or change.

Failing to identify a trend. However, even when you have a single comparison number, your insight is limited, because you can only determine whether you are over or under your target. A single number doesn't tell you whether this is a one-time incident or a continuing problem or trend. Real power comes from collecting metrics routinely and analyzing the *trend* of change from one period to another — this degree of change is sometimes called the "delta." A continuously decreasing trend in performance would indicate a true problem, while a single dip might be explained by an emergency, planned downtime, or other uncommon event.

Not being credible in the eyes of senior management. Another common error is the collection and preparation of metrics that are not credible in the eyes of senior management. Often, this error results because senior management was not consulted prior to the process of preparing the final metrics, while on other occasions it is because the metrics that are used by HR rely too heavily on soft measures. Sometimes, metrics lose credibility because management does not have faith in the accuracy of the data or information used to compile the metrics, and occasionally metrics are rejected because the numbers produced are just "too high to be believable."

If You Only Use One Metric — Here Is the "Ultimate Metric"

Throughout this book you will be provided with a variety of metrics that you can use to continually improve your performance. The ultimate metric (and the one I personally use and recommend) includes the following:

- You can't improve what you don't measure.

- You must compare "your" measures to the "quantified results" of the very best.

Then

- Be a better "you" … every day through continual learning.

- Beat your personal "yesterday's" results … every day.

- Beat your department's "yesterday's" results … every day.

- Beat where your competitor will be tomorrow … today (because the "best" are continually planning dramatic improvements).

- And, be paranoid that even the above won't be enough to stay on top … so don't get complacent, and consider aiming even higher!

Concluding Thoughts on Metrics

Words and actions *are never success measures,* but numbers and outputs are credible measures!

For HR to transform itself from its current role as a business partner and assume its rightful place as a business leader, the HR professional will have to adopt the language and the measurements of business. HR must be wise in selecting the measures it uses. And because acceptable ways of measuring are never defined by HR (but rather by finance, CEOs, customers, or the law), HR must primarily select its metrics from a list already used in business reporting throughout the firm.

That list includes these commonly utilized success measures:

- Return on investment

- Payback period

- Contribution to profit

- Increased productivity

- Increase in market share, competitive advantage, and/or customer satisfaction

- A cut in the time-to-market (product development time)

Now that you understand what a metric is and why you need to use metrics, and the difference between a good metric and a great one, the next step is understanding how they can be applied. Unless you are a senior manager in HR, it is unlikely that you will be asked to develop metrics for the whole department. As a result, the next few chapters highlight how metrics can be used in each of the major HR functions. Later in the book, you will find a chapter covering strategic HR metrics for the entire department.

Chapter Two
Staffing Metrics

2

Goal of this chapter

In the last chapter we learned the difference between a good and a great metric. This chapter is the first in a series of chapters outlining the appropriate metrics that can be used in each of the major independent HR functions. This chapter outlines recruiting and staffing strategies and the metrics that go with them. It contains a wide variety of metrics, tools, and checklists. Feel free to skip between the tools until you find the ones that best fit your needs.

What Managers Expect From Recruiting: Setting Performance Expectations Up Front

Staffing, like sales and manufacturing, is a production-oriented function for which it is fairly easy to develop metrics. There are clear inputs (applicants) and outputs (hires). However, despite the similarities with other input/output functions, few of the types of metrics that have driven sales and manufacturing for decades have been adopted within staffing. In fact, the only metric that is consistently used in recruiting is cost per hire (unlimited metric at best). As a result, the failure to use metrics has made managers unclear as to what they should expect from recruiting, and it has also made them more skeptical of recruiter performance. One of the ways to avoid these pitfalls is to talk directly to senior managers in order to identify their expectations up front.

To be highly successful in HR, we need to focus on the few things that give us a competitive advantage. Remember, almost 60% of all organizational costs are people costs, so leadership within Human Resources can have huge potential impact. And of all the HR functions, recruiting has one of the largest impacts. For example, if a hotel has a normal turnover rate (25 percent per year), it only takes two years of bad hiring before 50 percent of the employees are below par.

A lack of top talent impacts a firm's ability to grow, and in fact most businesses live or die based on their ability to attract and retain talent. Most of recruiting requires some degree of assessment. Whether we are assessing applicants, recruiting sources, or interview techniques, they all require metrics in order to identify what is working and what isn't. Because there are many legal implications in hiring, it is even more important to make sure we have metrics to back up whom we hire and whom we reject. Applicants and government agencies alike demand that we have systems that guarantee fairness and accuracy, and that requires data and metrics.

What Managers Say They Need from Staffing

For each of the following manager's needs, consider establishing metrics to track your performance.

- Flexibility — Managers need flexibility in exactly how they are allowed to recruit.

- Few rules — The more rules HR imposes, the less able managers are to respond to the changing environment.

- Excellent resumes — They can't waste too much of their time doing recruiting. Recruiting needs to provide managers with just a few great candidates and no weak ones.

- Training — Good managers are not automatically good recruiters — they need to be trained to be effective.

- Feedback — Managers need to know how well they are doing, so it's important to give managers feedback both from applicants who said yes and also from those who turned us down.

The Changing Economy — What This Means for Staffing

In the last few years, companies have gone from large-scale hiring to hiring freezes. Because the business environment and the demand for labor keep changing, it's important that staffing first change its approach and strategy to meet those changing needs. Some of the changes that staffing functions need to make include:

- We need to benchmark recruiting transaction cost against the best in the industry. Recruiting needs to increase its emphasis on the value-added side of recruiting, the quality (or the performance) of new hires.

- The growth areas in hiring are in service and support positions, and we need to get better in recruiting in those areas.

- We need to have a zero tolerance for bad performance within the recruiting function.

- Recruiting needs to anticipate and to develop viable pools of applicants who have "soon-to-be needed" skill sets well ahead of when they will be required.

- We need to send out an image and a brand to potential applicants that we are the "best place" to work.

- We need to be in a continuous search mode for top talent, because merely responding to job openings as they come in results in mediocre hiring.

- We need to eliminate functional structures and a lack of cooperation between HR functions if we are to improve recruiting.

- We need to break the culture of hiring people only of "like kind."

- We need to admit that some managers are just terrible at hiring.

- It is really hard, but HR has to learn how to say "no" to many good ideas and good people, and focus on a few important things.

Making the Business Case —
Why Managers Need to Pay Attention to Recruiting

One of the largest contributions that metrics can make to recruiting is to provide managers with data and numbers that convince them to spend more of their time on recruiting. If you want to go beyond emotional arguments, here are some economic factors or metrics that may get their attention.

- A recently hired "superstar" will produce as much as two times more than an average performer, and the very top superstar performers may produce as much as 10 times more.

- Hiring has the second-highest ROI (after retention) of any people practice.

- Customers can tell when a company hires great people (and poor ones). Vacancies send a message to customers that you don't care about them (because you hire weak people to work with them). Great hires increase customer satisfaction and result in more sales.

- On-time project completion will decrease by as much as one-third with key positions vacant.

- New hires bring new ideas and patents, and these new ideas can energize your team. Great hires increase your capability to expand your business and products. If you are in an industry that needs new ideas, hiring new talent is essential.

- Time-to-market and product development suffer the longer you have a vacancy (the cost of a vacancy in a key job is likely to be hundreds of thousands of dollars in revenue).

- Profits and productivity will go up as the proportion of "great hires" increases.

- Poor hires increase your error rates and require additional management time to "fix."

- Hiring great people gives you a competitive advantage and means that your competitor can't hire them!

- People decisions are the hardest decisions you will have to make. Developing great hiring practices will help you increase your manager's ability to make these and other tough decisions.

- Hiring "A" players will attract other "A" players (even in lower-level positions). Future recruiting is easy, once you have "A" players.

- Slow hiring sends a message to applicants that the firm is slow … which may impact your brand image and future sales.

- The reputation of slow or low-quality hiring sends a message to top management and other managers that you (an individual manager) are weak at "people management." This may impact your career.

- Recruiting and talking to candidates will increase your learning in other business areas. Recruiting keeps you "in touch" with the market. It will help you understand the needs and wants of your candidates, as well as increase your "sales" ability and your offer-acceptance rates.

- The cost of a "bad hire," on average is three times their salary. The very worst hire may cause damage that exceeds their salary by over 10 times.

A Checklist for Assessing Your Recruiting Tools and Practices: A Quick Audit

You can do a quick "audit" to see if your employment function is "part of the problem or part of the solution"! You are not on your way toward a world-class employment function if you cannot answer "yes" to at least ten of these thirteen items:

1. Do you have a continuously updated competitive analysis of your direct competitors' employment practices?

2. Do you reward your managers with a direct bonus of at least 5% for great attraction and retention?

3. Do you track and show the performance (success) of the employees you hire and report it to managers?

4. Do you track and reward recruiters directly for great (high-performing) hires?

5. Do you get more than 50% of your hires from referrals?

6. Do you spend more of your employment budget on Web recruiting than on "paper want ads"?

7. Do you do periodic "profiles" of your target candidates so that you know their job acceptance criteria as well as what they read, the sites they surf, and their interests?

8. Do you coordinate employment activities with PR and marketing efforts?

9. Do line managers "own" and do more than 50% of all recruiting tasks?

10. Do you not require a "requisition," a resume, and multiple interviews to generate a hire?

11. Does your time to fill (make a hiring decision) take less than 30 days for key positions?

12. Do you prioritize service to jobs and hiring managers based on the forecasted impact of the position?

13. Does a survey of your line managers show that at least 50% know the name and the key elements of your employment strategy?

A Checklist for Assessing Your Employment Strategy: Common Errors to Avoid

In the last section, we found a checklist that allowed us to look at how effectively we utilize the latest recruiting tools and practices tools. In this section, the checklist is focused on the broader recruiting strategy. It lists the common errors or weaknesses in most employment strategies. Utilize it to see if your overall recruiting strategy has weaknesses.

- The recruiting plan is not tied into the business plan

- There is no written recruiting plan

- There is no competitive analysis comparing what we do to what others do

- Strategy doesn't have a name that is well known internally

- Goals are not prioritized and quantified

- No results metrics are included (especially quality of hire and quality of source)

- No rewards for managers (and recruiters) for great hiring/retention

- No link to other external (and internal) databases and HR programs

- No emphasis on measuring or improving the quality of the hire

- Weak branding strategy

- Weak referral program

- No retention component

- Positions and managers are not prioritized so that resources can be better allocated toward high priority areas

- No continuous improvement component is built into the strategy

- No customer/applicant satisfaction measurement component

- Doesn't include a "firing" component for getting rid of "bad" hires

- Too much focus on "actives" (currently employed people) and hiring strangers

- No global or 24/7 availability

- It takes a primarily reactive vs. proactive (anticipatory) approach to problems

- No or a weak component designed to influence line managers, teams, and employees to take "ownership" of the employment process and to raise its priority to the highest level

- Failure to replace traditional recruiters with the employees that have headhunter attitude and a marketing focus

- Failure to coordinate employment activities with PR and marketing efforts

- The strategy is not technology-focused (paperless, remote assessment, and the hiring manager has desktop access to all employment tools and metrics)

- No clear plan demonstrating what activities we want more of and less of

Steps in Developing a Plan for Transforming into a World-Class Employment Function

The last two sections provided brief checklists on how to assess your use of recruiting tools and your employment strategy. This next section goes into a little more depth by providing some steps to take to transform your "average" recruiting function into a world-class one.

What are the baseline principles for a world-class employment function? First, before an employment function can become world-class, both HR and the firm must be driven by a competitive advantage mentality. The company and HR must have a performance culture whose goal is dominance in their industry through the attraction and retention of the most productive employees. A competitive advantage can be maintained only by beating the performance of our top competitors in each and every employment subfunction and then by improving it at a rate so fast that the competitor cannot catch up.

Employment's next step toward becoming world-class is to get managers and employees to raise the priority they put (percent of time spent) on recruiting. You need to attract the best employees to win, and that is not possible without the involvement of everyone!

Next, staffing must have multiple tools and approaches to recruiting, because it takes a different approach in every situation to get and retain the very best talent. Tools that work for secretaries may not work for IT professionals. Without numerical proof, you should assume that all employment practices are ineffective and need to be replaced with higher-return or more effective tools.

The next step is to assume that all recruiting is marketing, and a marketing-based strategy is the foundation of everything we do. The best recruiting functions constantly learn from the sales and marketing function

Performance metrics and incentives must drive all aspects of the staffing function. It is essential that we demonstrate our value to managers in performance, dollars, and ROI.

Senior management must implement the rule that excellence in people management (including recruitment) is a condition of employment for all line managers, because "C"-quality managers can't/won't hire "A"-quality employees. Managers who can't hire great people … need to be replaced.

The employment manager must establish that employment practices are not "sacred cows" and that every process, program, or system that can't prove it gives us a competitive advantage will be dropped, outsourced, or dramatically improved.

Employment must shift its approach and begin to act in a role similar to that of a "financial advisor"! Our staff will give advice and do risk analysis, but they will not be an HR "cop" — nor will they "own" hiring. Within a range, managers must be given discretion to control how/whom they hire and then be held accountable for their results.

Employment must be forward-looking. It will forecast and anticipate. Managers must be forward-looking and begin to aim at a moving target six months in advance of where we are now. Managers can never be satisfied that where we are today is "good enough."

Next, the employment function must hire and train the best recruiters and employment staff, and then reward them heavily for success.

And the final step must be that the same vigor and resources must be placed on the internal "redeployment of talent" as are dedicated to external recruiting.

Are You an Employer of Choice?
Metrics for Assessing Your Progress

It has become common for firms to strive to become an "employer of choice" (EOC). An employer of choice is not a formal designation. But it can be measured. Generally, an employer of choice is a company that is either listed as one in a major publication or a company that is mentioned in the top five choices when a top performer (and potential candidate) is asked, "What is your dream firm to work at?"

Unfortunately, it's easy to say that you have become an employer of choice. In reality, though, being an employer of choice is a difficult albeit measurable status to obtain. Here are some ways to assess how far you have come in the EOC sweepstakes. The EOC factors are listed here in descending order of importance.

1. **"Best" list appearances.** The firm currently appears on *Fortune*'s or *Working Mother*'s best places list and on more than one industry or regional best places list.

2. **Positive name recognition in target population.** When asked in a survey or focus group, people in your target professional fields know the name of your firm 75% of the time, and over half of those know at least one key positive selling point of your firm.

3. **In the top three choices of top performers.** When highly qualified professionals are asked the names of places they "would like to work someday," over 50% list your firm in the top five most often mentioned.

4. **Where your applications come from.** At least 10% of your applicants come from the top five most profitable firms in your industry or region.

5. **Often cited in MVPs.** Your firm's HR and people practices are cited at least five times a year by name in the top three (most

valuable publications) that are read by top professionals in their field or industry.

6. **Often cited.** Your firm's HR and people practices are cited by name in major industry, business, and HR publications over 50 times a year.

7. **Referral rate.** Employee referrals make up over 50% of all hires.

8. **"Other offers."** Applicants with multiple offers also get a concurrent offer from one of the top ten—rated firms in your industry at least 50% of the time.

9. **Give away/take away ratio.** Your firm hires away more people from your top five competitors than the competitor hires away from you (you win four out of five of these head-to-head battles).

10. **Talent competitors talk positively about you.** When managers at direct talent competitors are asked in surveys or focus groups about your firm's people practices, they give a positive response 25% of the time.

11. **In top three choices of average performers.** When professionals in your industry are asked the names of places they "would like to work someday," over 25% list your firm.

12. **Recruiters list you in top employers.** When professional recruiters are asked in surveys or focus groups about your firm's people practices, they give a positive response 50% of the time. When asked to list the top ten EOCs in your region or industry, they cite you 50% of the time.

13. **On "admired" list.** You appear on *Fortune*'s "most admired firms" list.

14. **On diversity list.** You appear on *Fortune*'s diversity list.

15. **Former employees do/would return.** Over 10% of employees who voluntarily quit in the past three years have returned. Over 50% express an interest in returning when surveyed.

16. **Employees send the "same" message.** When your employees are asked what they tell strangers about "why the firm is a great place to work," over 50% of their answers include your top selling point.

17. **Low turnover rate of top performers.** The turnover rate of your top 25%–rated employees is below 5%.

18. **CEO mentions people practices.** Your current CEO mentions specific HR or people practices by name in 25% of external and 50% of internal speeches.

19. **Sign-up lists.** Your "sign-ups" at college information events exceed the average by 50%. Your lines at job fairs are 25% longer than your top direct talent competitor.

20. **Web hits.** You get 50% more Web hits on your jobs page than the industry average.

21. **Benchmarked.** *Fortune* 500 firms from outside your industry benchmark you (call to learn about your best practices) at least once a year.

22. **Listed first in conference brochures.** When presenting firms are listed in commercial seminar brochures, your firm's name appears in the first 25%.

23. **Book.** There has been a book written about your firm or CEO within the last five years.

24. **CEO has wide name recognition.** Your current CEO has a *positive* name recognition 75% of the time when professionals in your industry are asked to comment in surveys or focus groups.

25. **You have an EOC manager.** Your HR department has a designated EOC, best places list, or employment branding manager.

Conclusion: HR loses all credibility when it overuses phrases like "we are an employer of choice," when in fact it has no hard data to back up the assertion. Wise HR VPs will demand that EOC progress be measured with metrics and numbers, rather than wishful thinking!

Introduction to "Quality of Hire" — What Is a "Better Hire"?

The most underutilized metric in recruiting is "quality of hire. The quality of hire simply means that the performance of the newly hired individual on the job (within six to 12 months of hire) will clearly exceed the performance of the "average hire." In brief, increasing the quality of hire means measuring that performance differential between the new hires and the average worker. This section is the first of four parts, which will highlight what a quality hire is and how to measure it.

Everyone wants to improve the results of their hiring process. But what is a "better hire"? That's a good question, and one which many HR practitioners have had difficulty in defining. The consensus is that a "better hire" is someone who meets most of the criteria listed below.

Measurement checklist for a "better hire"
A candidate or new hire is a "better hire" when they:

- Have more competencies/skills (both competencies that we need now and that we will need in the future). And as a result, they require less training.

- Are agile, can multitask, and can shift rapidly to new problems and jobs.

- Are rapid learners and will self-develop, and are continuously learning individuals who will do so without the need for company training.

- Have more ideas that are implemented and that impact your profitability.

- Require "low maintenance" from managers. These employees have a lower error rate, number of disciplinary incidents, and absenteeism rate than other employees.

- Have a higher customer satisfaction rating, higher performance-appraisal scores, and higher bonus rates, forced-ranking scores, and promotion rates.

- Inspire and train others to be more productive.

- Stay longer before quitting.

- Produce more return for every dollar of salary paid them.

- Have a sense of urgency and continually improve all systems and people they manage.

- Are forward-focused, and monitor and accurately forecast the environment.

- Know how to prove business results through metrics.

How and When to Measure Quality of Hire

In the last section, you were provided with a checklist of the factors that made someone a "better hire." Here, I'll introduce a quick checklist for assessing the quality of your hires. In the following section, there is an outline and how to measure the quality of your applicants. And in the fourth and final section, there is a list of reasons why you should stop focusing on the traditional "cost of hire" metric.

One thing that you should remember is that if your organization is hiring hundreds of people, you might want to consider measuring the quality of hire by using a random sample of new hires instead of trying to assess everyone.

What should you measure for quality of hire?

There are a variety of approaches to measuring the quality of your hires. Here's a list of five of the broad categories along with actual metrics you can use in each.

1. **Individual performance metrics.** Individual performance metrics help you determine if the people you hired this year outperformed those hired last year (in their job classification).

    Actual metrics:
    *   On-the-job performance: Productivity, output, sales volume, customer satisfaction scores, efficiency, etc.
    *   Number of weeks until they reach the (preset) minimal acceptable level of productivity
    *   Their average bonus/pay for performance rewards (the percentage of their total salary rewarded in bonuses)
    *   Error rates
    *   Customer service scores
    *   Scores on forced rankings, 360-degree feedback, etc.
    *   Their performance appraisal scores (for similar jobs)
    *   The number of months until they are promoted (with a lower number being better)

- The number of company awards, recognitions, or nominations
- Higher percentage salary increases (as a percentage of salary, where salary is related to performance)
- Performance on training and assessment tests or in classes

2. **Retention rates of new hires.** This is a metric you can use to determine if the percentage of hires who are still with the firm after one year is higher this year than last.

   Actual metrics:
   - Compare the new hire voluntary termination rates for top performers and key jobs from one year to the next. Adjust for any "inflation" in overall industry retention rates (or compare this year's rate to last)
   - Compare the new hire voluntary termination rates for all hires from one year to the next. Adjust for any "inflation" in overall industry retention rates (or compare this year's rate to last)

3. **Manager satisfaction.** This is done through surveys of hiring managers to show if there is a significantly higher satisfaction rate with the recruiting process this year as compared to last.

   Actual metrics: Look at hiring managers' satisfaction with —
   - The quality (competencies) of the hire
   - The quality of the recruiter's responsiveness to managers' requests
   - Response time to manager requests
   - The number of hires
   - The job performance of the hire
   - The diversity of the hire
   - The number and severity of legal issues and problems as a result of the hiring process

4. **Applicant satisfaction.** Surveys of applicants can show if there is a significantly higher rate of satisfaction with how they were treated during the recruiting process — again, this year compared to last. Because rejected applicants may someday be customers, you need to ensure that they are treated well.

    Actual metrics: Look at applicants' satisfaction with —
    *   The way the recruiter treated them
    *   The recruitment process
    *   The firm (Has the firm's image improved as a result of the recruiting effort?)
    *   The product (Has the image of the firm's products changed as a result of the recruiting effort?)

5. **Cost of the hire.** Are the starting salaries (adjusted for inflation) for this year's hires the same or lower than last year's?

    Actual metrics:
    *   Compare accepted offers, adjusted for salary inflation, within position classifications for this year compared to last year to see if you are "over-offering" in order to get candidates to say yes.

When to measure the quality of hire

Following is a list of possible quality-of-hire measures, ordered by when to measure them. As a general rule, the more powerful measures are listed first in each section. Results and output measures are always superior to other assessments.

1. **Immediate measures** (i.e., on the day of hire)

   - Did the actual hire's resume rank in the top 25% (e.g., did it receive an A or A+) when the initial resumes were assessed/ranked?
   - Percentage of qualifications on final job description that this candidate met (including number of years of experience and education the hire has compared to the requisition and other recent hires).
   - When the initial finalists for the job were forced-ranked after interviews, but prior to an offer, what rank was the actual hire among those finalists?
   - Did the actual hire also get offers from your top-ranked recruiting competitors?
   - Manager's prediction of the quality of hire (based on a subjective comparison against other recent hires). What percentile do they forecast their performance level to be at?
   - Manager's forced-ranking comparison of this candidate compared to other recent hires.
   - Manager's satisfaction with the hiring process (responsiveness, cost, time, etc.).
   - Surveys of new hire satisfaction with how they were treated during the hiring process by the recruiter, this year compared to last.
   - Surveys of new hire satisfaction on how they were treated during the hiring process by the hiring manager, this year compared to last.

- Time from contact about this job to hire date.
- Satisfaction of the other finalists (who were not selected) with the hiring process.

2. **Intermediate measures** (up to six months after hire)

   - Output or production (quality and quantity) compared to other recent hires as well as the overall employee average after one month and at six months (e.g., productivity, output, sales volume, percentage of projects completed, customer satisfaction scores, etc.).
   - Manager's subjective assessment of performance of the hire after one month and at 6 months.
   - Team and co-worker subjective assessment of performance of the hire after one month and at six months.
   - Time to productivity (i.e., the number of days until the minimum expected output level is reached for a new hire).
   - How well new hires do on any required testing, certifications, or training, this year compared to last.
   - Satisfaction of the new hire after one month.
   - The quality of your applicants.
   - Legal complaints or issues.

3. **Longer-term assessment** (over one year)

   - Output and results (quality and quantity) compared to other recent hires as well as the overall employee average after one year (e.g., productivity, output, sales volume, percentage of projects completed, customer satisfaction scores, etc.).
   - Manager's assessment of performance of the hire at their one-year performance evaluation.
   - Year-end surveys of all hiring managers on satisfaction with the recruiting process, this year compared to last.

- The percentage of above-average performers who are still with the firm (excluding terminations) after one year, this year compared to last (be sure to adjust for any "inflation" in overall industry retention rates).
- Customer 360-degree feedback or complaints, satisfaction, or other assessments.
- Co-worker and team 360-degree feedback (or forced ranking) of new hires, this year compared to last).
- Manager's forced ranking of this hire compared to others in the same job.
- Average performance appraisal (or forced ranking score) of this year's hires versus last year's.
- Percentage of stock grants compared to other recent hires and all employees.
- Number and dollar value of any "spot" and year-end bonuses (as a percentage of salary) compared to other hires and all employees.
- Number of nominations/awards compared to other hires and all employees.
- Number of salary increases compared to other hires and all employees.
- Number of months until they are promoted or receive a grade increase (with a lower number being better) compared to other hires and all employees.
- Number of lateral transfers compared to other hires and all employees.
- Number of patents/ideas compared to other hires and all employees.
- Cost of their salary: How do the starting salaries (adjusted for inflation) for this year's hires compare to last year's for employees rated at the same level of performance?

Overall assessment of the quality of your workforce

An overall assessment of the quality of your workforce should be done each year. Take a step back and look at these "big picture" items:

- Revenue per employee compared to your direct competitors, as a "mirror" of the quality of your people

- Dollars of profit per dollar spent on people costs (this year to last, and also compared to your direct competitors)

- Survey of local recruiters and executive search professionals on how you rank in quality of recruiting and hires (survey should be conducted by HR advertising or market research firms)

- How you are listed on great-place-to-work lists

- How often you appear on benchmark lists for great recruiting

Conclusion

Now that you know the quality of your hires, the next steps are to identify:

- The sources the best came from (so you can drop the "useless" ones)

- The factors in the selection process that gave them high and low scores (so that you can drop the measures that don't predict success)

- The recruiters/managers/employees who found them (so you can reward them and use them again)

And last … change the reward system for managers and recruiters so that the quality of the hire is the main reward focus.

If you have generated some numbers but are unsure how good your numbers are, try the Saratoga Institute or www.staffing.org. Both organizations specialize in HR benchmark data collection.

Once you implement a quality-of-hire measure, don't be surprised when many of the traditional things that you used to measure become irrelevant. You might also stop "feeling good" when you have filled all of your requirements, because now you also need to focus on bringing in better people who become top performers in your organization!

If I haven't answered all of your questions in this book, I suggest that you drop by and talk to the supply chain or Six Sigma experts at your firm. They are light-years ahead of HR in measuring the "hard stuff," and can easily tell you what else you need to know.

Remember, you can't improve what you do not measure!

How to Measure the Quality of Your Applicants (Before You Hire Them)

Managers are continually asking for a higher quality of candidate while recruiters tend to focus on the cost or the speed of the hire. The quality of the applicant is clearly the superior factor. There are many ways to measure the quality of the applicants (before you hire them). Some of them include:

- They get at least one counter offer — If they are any good (unless they work for government or a not-for-profit) their current boss will give them at least one counteroffer to match yours. The very top get two.

- They are currently employed — In low unemployment times, if they are not currently working, odds are that they are not top talent.

- They have three offers from top firms — In high employment times, if they are active job seekers, the very best have multiple job offers and at least one from a top firm. If yours have only one offer (yours), they are not top talent (unless you live in a single employer area).

- Our top performers know them — If we are any good, our top people know them. Top performers are a hard secret to keep.

- Executive search professionals know them — Professionals we work with have them in their database.

- They were hard to convince — Because the best are in demand, they are hard to "sell." If they don't have high expectations and they settle easily, something is wrong (or you did great market research).

- They fit our competency profile — They have at least 110% of the competencies that our specs cover. They have skills and experiences that are not in our minimum requirements.

- They are gone quickly — The best are taken rapidly. If we are slow to make a decision and they are still around after 10 days, they are not top talent (or you are the employer of choice for the region).

- Awards — Top performers are publicly recognized in their firms. They might also be highly rewarded in monetary terms also (a >10% raise or a >20% bonus).

- Manager satisfaction — If you survey your hiring managers on their satisfaction with the quality of the applicants they receive, you can get an idea of their assessment of the quality.

- This year's vs. last — Select a random number of applicants' resumes from this year and last (in the same job). Mix them up and have an expert anonymously select the top and bottom 20%. See whether this year's applicants are better represented in the top category.

- The source — If a current top performer referred them, odds are that they are also a top performer. Referrals consistently rate as the highest-quality applicants.

Don't be fooled

Traditional measures of quality might be misleading. Be careful of:

Resume quality — Top performers seldom have great or even current resumes. People who are on the job market a long time have time to polish and improve their resumes. Be aware that many people don't even write their own resume!

Schools attended — Top performers come from many schools. The best usually do excel at whatever school they went to. Don't assume. Check to see where your firm's top performers actually went.

Grades — In a diverse world where many students are older or have to work, overall GPA might not predict much. Grades in their major might show more. See if your current top performers had great grades first.

Number of years of experience — In a rapidly changing world, information and technology change rapidly, so "experience" in a dated technology might mean little.

Stop Measuring the Cost of Hire: It's Not a Strategic Measure

HR professionals often say that they want to be strategic, but their actions indicate otherwise. Take the all-too-commonly-used "cost per hire" metric. Sure, it's used by lots of people — but so is astrology. It's relatively easy to cut the cost of a hire (hire walk-ins or the homeless at your doorstep, for example), but the impacts on the business will probably mean that you are being "penny wise and pound foolish." Let me explain what's wrong with cost per hire (CPH), and how it can be supplemented with the "quality" of a hire metric.

What's wrong with cost per hire?

The following is a long list of some of the reasons you should reduce the emphasis on CPH:

- Relatively speaking, the amount spent on a hire is "chump change." A major firm may have "revenue per employee" of $600,000, while its cost of a hire is only around $10,000. $10k compared to $600k is not much. In addition, if the person you hired becomes a top-ranked performer (as opposed to an average one), the difference in the "revenue" generated over three years might be nearly a million dollars! (Remember, top-ranked performers often generate over 50% more revenue than average ones.) It's the return on the investment that is the important thing to measure — not the amount (cost) of the investment!

- Hiring cheap is easy. Finding a great person is never easy or cheap. Employed top performers are more difficult and expensive to recruit. Hiring walk-ins and poor-quality applicants "no one wants" is cheap but not smart.

- Quality is usually expensive. The metric "cost per hire" often does not have the corresponding metric attached: the "quality or performance of the hire." Hiring "Michael Jordan" is time-consuming and requires a great deal of looking, management time, and schmoozing, all of which cost money. If too much emphasis is placed on cost-cutting, HR might get into the bad habit of "hiring cheap." Web development is expensive, but it may bring in more top performers per dollar spent than cheaper tools such as a job fair.

- If you hire a high performer (high sales, output, productivity, or performance-appraisal scores), their higher productivity (usually three to seven times salary) will make the cost of their hire insignificant in comparison. Hiring low performers is cheap and easy. The competition for the top people drives up the costs of convincing and hiring them.

- Provide the CEO with evidence of the high performance/productivity of those you hire, and the cost will not be an issue. Great HR people try to improve revenue and output rather than cut costs. Hiring "no one" is cheap, but it will not increase revenue or help develop a better product!

- Cheap hiring sends a cheap message. Recruits (especially "Michael Jordan" types) judge a company by their ads, Web pages, and so forth. Being "cheap" might send a clear message to applicants that you are on the way down. Trying to cut your cost of hire you may actually increase your costs by scaring away many applicants with a "cheap message." "Kmart" advertising doesn't attract "Tiffany" customers!

- Cheap hiring might mean poor service. Most hiring measures fail to include a customer service assessment metric. If there are no metrics on how satisfied managers and applicants are with the recruitment and selection process, you cannot tell if your cost-cutting is frustrating your managers and applicants with poor customer service. If applicants are also likely to be customers, this is a strategic error that may cost you more in sales than in the dollars you saved in cut-rate recruiting.

- Cheap hiring is slow. Cutting cost almost always slows up the "speed of the hire." If your "time-to-market" is a business issue, then cutting HR costs might actually raise your costs in product development and production — which means a possible cut in the resulting product margins and market share.

- It's only 2%. The average cost of a hire is generally in the $3,000 to $5,000 range. That is usually less than 10% of a first-year salary of $45k. If the person stays for an average of three years and you include benefits costs, then the actual cost of a hire becomes roughly 2% of the total dollars paid to the employee.

What is the "Quality of Hire"?

Costs are generally not strategic without the corresponding quality measures to go with them. Instead of costs, calculate the rate of return on recruiting dollars spent, and if the return is high enough, your CEO might want you to actually spend more on recruiting!

Conclusion

One of the best ways to improve a company is to begin to recruit quality people who produce more per dollar of salary paid than those hired the preceding year (and who produce more per dollar spent on them than people hired by the competitors).

The next step is to forget the cost per hire as a primary metric. Don't ignore costs, but you might have to spend more money to get great people. Do you really think that the CEO would care about such a small cost item as cost per hire if you hired someone as good as "Michael Jordan"? Remember, the cost of driving a mile in a Yugo is lower then driving a mile in a BMW ... but if you watch costs too closely, you might end up walking home after your Yugo breaks down!

Now don't get me wrong. It's important to measure the effectiveness of all recruiting and staffing tools and to drop the ineffective ones. Just don't do it to save money. Do it in order to hire better people! It's like trying to save money on your own upcoming brain surgery operation — probably not a great strategic move!

Hiring quality candidates requires both great recruiting tools and speed. Unfortunately, most recruiting managers are unwilling to spend the time and resources necessary to streamline hiring processes until they understand the dollar cost of a long-term position vacancy. The next section outlines how to calculate the cost of vacancy.

Calculating the Cost of a Vacant Position
(A List of the Possible "COV" Factors)

If an airline bought a new 767, and then let it sit for two months on the runway because they didn't have a pilot, what would the cost be to the airline? In other words, what is the cost of a vacant position?

Many firms calculate the cost of hire, and some go as far as to calculate the cost of bad hire, but few have taken the time to calculate the cost of vacant position. The costs can be significant: anywhere from $7,000 to $50,000 per day for an average *Fortune* 500 position. Key leadership positions may cost as much as a million dollars per week. Couple these amounts with the fact that the time length of many vacancies often exceeds 100 days, and you are talking some serious financial impacts ($7k x 100 days = $700k).

Although I've done a great number of these cost-of-vacancy (COV) calculations, I have generally found that the results are less "believable" when the calculations are done by outsiders or by HR professionals. Instead, I have had better luck when line managers do the actual calculation (even though the numbers might be off some). Also, the results are more likely to be used by managers to put pressure on retention programs and on speeding up the recruiting and hiring process.

Assumptions About Vacancies

Delaying product development and time-to-market in a fast-changing industry means:

- Lower margins (as much as 10%)

- A loss of first-entry dominance

- A loss of PR

- Potential loss of market share (up to 30%)

Great ideas and products come from people — not from equipment, buildings, or capital. If you don't have great people, you won't have great products. And without great products, you won't have a great company.

If the vacancies are a result of a slow recruiting process, it is important to also realize that a failure to fill vacancies rapidly will probably also mean that all of the top candidates will be gone by the time you make a hiring decision. So you will likely refill your vacancies with lower-quality hires (especially because the best are usually the first to quit).

Vacancies in a single team can have an impact on many other teams (because of interdependencies), an effect which can cascade throughout an entire company.

Cost of a Vacancy Checklist: The Business Impacts of a Vacancy

When you have a vacant position, one or more of the following things may happen. Try guesstimating the dollar costs of each bullet point that fits your situation.

Product Development and Productivity

- Time-to-market (TTM) is dramatically impacted by the entire production chain. Because departmental schedules and plans are closely interwoven, any disruption in one department may adversely affect all others.

- In industries that are seasonal (e.g., toys), this disruption may be even more costly. Vacancies in key skill positions may mean that products and projects may need to be dropped altogether.

Team Impacts

- Team product development may be dramatically impacted by the disruption caused by the lost productivity, experience, leadership, idea generation, and skills of the "vacated" person.

- Vacancies may affect the idea generation of others, because co-workers are frustrated or overworked.

- Vacancies may cause overworked employees (because they have to fill in) to tire, which may cause increased accidents.

- Vacancies may cause overworked employees to tire, which may adversely affect product quality through increased error rates.

- Excessive vacancies may lead to increased "whining," grievances, and even union activity.

Individual Employee Impacts

- A vacancy means that a current employee must do the work of the vacant position. This can create a cascading effect, causing others to have to fill in for "their" position, resulting in many "rusty" people doing unfamiliar jobs — and decreasing productivity.

- Vacancies may frustrate other employees, causing them to lower their productivity.

- Vacancies may frustrate other employees, causing them to quit at a higher rate than they normally would.

- Vacancies may cause the team to miss its goals, thereby reducing the possibility of individual and team incentives, which may further reduce productivity.

- Superstar employees often resent being asked to fill in when lesser employees' positions are vacant, which may cause them to quit also.

Increased Management Time and Effort

- Teams with vacancies require "high maintenance" and more management attention and worry.

- Managers often have to skip their normal management planning and responsibilities in order to fill in for the vacant employee.

- When managers fill in for "vacant" employees, that time can't be spent on the best employees.

- Vacancies in management and team leader positions have a multiplier effect on productivity and the recruitment of others.

- There are opportunity costs for things a manager and co-workers could have done if they didn't have to carry the extra load of filling in for a vacancy.

- If the vacancies are caused by top management decisions (hiring or budget freezes), managers can lose hope. This can impact morale, and it may lead to a high management turnover rate.

Customer Impacts

- Excessive vacancies may send a message to customers and suppliers that we are getting weak or that we don't care about them. It may cause a period of confusion for suppliers and customers regarding whom they can contact and the stability of the relationship. Errors caused by "vacant" employees may lose sales volume and occasionally customers.

- Any "fill-in" as a sales/account rep may provide customers an opportunity or excuse to look for other suppliers.

Our Competitive Advantage

- Vacancies at the CEO, CFO, CTO, and other top manager positions can adversely impact our financing and the willingness of others to partner/merge with us.

- Vacancies in key positions may send a message to analysts and the stock market that we are getting weak.

- Vacancies may send a message to competitors that we are vulnerable, which can lead to increased competitive pressures.

Our Image and Recruiting

- Excessive vacancies send a message to our competitors that we are getting weak. This might encourage them and improve their own confidence such that they become bolder in the product- and employee-poaching market.

- Vacancies may impact new recruiting, because vacancies send a message to future recruits that we are not easily able to recruit replacements.

- Large numbers of vacancies may also send a message to our current employees that we are headed downhill.

- High vacancy rates may overstress our recruiters and recruitment process.

- Vacancies may send a message to outside recruiters that we are vulnerable, which can lead to increased "headhunter" activity.

Out-of-Pocket Costs

- Having to hire high-cost consultants as "fill-in help" could mean higher costs. If hourly employees are involved, it probably means additional overtime costs.

- Vacancies can mean the underutilization of plant and equipment.

Other Miscellaneous Concerns (and Costs) That May Arise

- The new hire may be a lower-quality (low-performance) candidate.

- New hires are unlikely to be immediately productive, thus resulting in increased costs.

- Some "vacating employees" take others with them soon after they leave. A "break in the dike" caused by one leaving may cause the whole intact team to leave.

- Many new hires don't work out and must be replaced within six months, essentially stretching the length of the vacancy.

- In a tight labor market, vacancies in hard-to-hire jobs may not be fillable at any cost.

- In start-ups and small departments where there may be little cross-training, the cost may be even more dramatic. If you have only ten employees and then lose two, you have a 20 percent vacancy rate.

- Spending the time to avoid vacancies may have a huge ROI, especially if our former employees go to a competitor and take "our" ideas with them — causing the competitor's revenues to increase as ours go down.

After calculating the high cost of having a vacancy, most recruiting managers shift their efforts towards streamlining the hiring process. Another popular course of action is then to decide that all new hires or positions should be treated equally. Many HR professionals and managers resist this "prioritization" unless they are shown the business case that demonstrates the differential in value between hiring top performers and average ones. The steps in calculating the value of top performers are covered in the next two sections.

Calculating the Value of Hiring and Retaining Top Performers (Dollar Difference in Output for Top Performers)

Identifying the dollar value of top performers when compared with average workers isn't hard to do. Start with identifying some jobs with measurable results — sales-related positions are a great starting point. Then look at other roles that still have easily measured outputs, such as programmers (lines of code) or customer service reps. Next, you compare the differences in output between those individuals ranked as average performers and those ranked as the best. Here is how it can be done on a step-by-step basis:

1. Determine the output of the average and top performer. Start with the output of the average performer. This is called the average output per employee. Then look at the output of the very top performer (or the average of the top 1%). This is called the top performer output.

2. Calculate the top performer increase factor. Start with the top performer output per employee as the base. Then divide into that number the output of the average performer (the small number into the bigger number). That is the top performer increase factor.

3. Determine revenue per employee. Calculate the average revenue for an employee for these jobs (total revenue of the firm for a year divided by the number of employees).

4. Calculate the revenue increase for top performers. Take the average revenue per employee and multiply it by the top performer increase factor. That number is the revenue generated by a top performer.

5. Calculate the value difference between top and average performers. Subtract the average revenue per employee from the revenue of a top performer. The difference is the value added each year by hiring or retaining a top performer.

Add additional jobs. Next, do this for other measurable output jobs. If the ratio (the percent difference) is close for most jobs (it usually is), use that ratio for all jobs in the firm.

Example

The average salesperson has an annual sales volume (output) of $250,000. The top performer in the same group has an annual volume of $750,000. By dividing the output of the average performer into that of the top performer, we find that the top performer increase factor is 3.

During the last four completed quarters, the company has generated $350M, and had an average employee head count of 1,000, resulting in $350,000 in revenue per employee. By taking the revenue per employee of $350,000 and multiplying by the top performer increase factor of 3, we see that the average revenue contributed by top performers is $1.05M. Subtracting the average revenue per employee from this number yields, on average, that top performers contribute $700,000 more each year than average performers. If you hire or retain ten of these top performers, you increase the revenue of the firm by $7M per year.

Advanced Variations

- Profit per employee. You can substitute total dollars of profit for total revenue and get profit for top performers.

- People profit (profit per employee dollar spent). Substitute total dollars of profit for total revenue dollars. AND substitute dollars paid for all employees (all salary, benefits, and training and HR costs) for the number of employees.

- Profit per employee. You can substitute total dollars of profit for total revenue and get profit for top performers.

- People profit increase by top performers. Take the total dollars of profit and divide it by the dollars paid for all employees (all salary, benefits, and training). This gives you profit per dollar of employee costs. Then multiply it by the top performer increase factor (#5 above). The difference between the top and the average is the profit per dollar of employee cost differential for top employees.

More Options

If actual jobs can't be used, consider another (or a combination of) "mirror" measure(s). For example:

- Evaluate actual events when a top performer left/joined and where a noticeable differential in performance (either individual or business unit) occurred. (The reverse is true with a bottom performer.)

- Try using the normal "bell" curve differential as a guide.

- Look at sports performance differentials (usually five to ten times) as a "mirror" of what happens in business (where performance and pay are public information).

- Look at the current bonus allocation to see differentials.

- Look at the current pay differentials to identify variances.

- Look at customer ratings to identify variances (forced distribution).

- Look at training ratings, assessment centers, or test scores to identify variances.

- Look at the 80/20 rule of profit from top-performing products to identify similar variances.

- Look at error or quality rates to identify variances (forced distribution).

- Get recruiters or headhunters to assess their market value differential.

- Use Bill Gates's estimate of 100 times.

- Look at the actual dollar differential assessments made by other firms (Adobe, Intel, Microsoft, Cisco, Agilent) of between three and ten times.

- Look at studies done by consulting firms (Watson Wyatt, McKinsey).

- Get the CFO/CEO to make a guesstimate.

Top Performers Are a Bargain — The Business Case for Hiring the Best

Are top performers expensive? If you ask any expert in compensation to tell you what the typical pay differential (i.e., salary and bonus) is between an average performer and a top performer in the same job, you might be surprised to find out that the differential isn't much.

The analysis goes something like this:

Top performers can be paid slightly more

- Top performers generally do get paid more than average performers. But the extra compensation for top performers rarely exceeds 40% over what average workers get in the same job.

Top performers may cost no more than average performers

- In some situations, the pay differential between a top and average performer may actually be a negative number. In other words, top performers may get paid less than average performers. For example, universities, government agencies, and other unionized organizations may actually compensate an individual who outperforms other workers less because of their lack of seniority or because they have been out of school for a shorter period of time than their "seasoned" counterparts. They also may get paid exactly the same because there is no performance bonus program.

- Since benefits are not based on performance, there are no additional benefit costs when hiring a top performer.

- Top performers require no more management time, training (they may actually require less), or travel expenses than average performers.

- Top performers require no unique or additional equipment.

- The cost of recruiting a top performer is, in most cases, no higher than for hiring an average performer.

So what does this all mean?

What it means is that when you calculate the difference in total costs (including all of the above-listed factors) of managing the employee from hire to termination, the actual net cost of hiring a top performer is generally no more than 25% higher than the cost of hiring an average performer.

Asking the important question: If I spend more, do I get more?

Given this scenario, any reasonable CFO would ask the following question: "If top performers cost only 25% more, do they produce at least 25% more?" In other words, what is the performance differential between top performers and average performers, and does that performance differential warrant spending 25% more to hire and retain a top performer versus an average performer?

And now the revelation …

Top performers, by definition, do perform at a higher level than average performers. The revelation here is that top performers almost always exceed the performance of average workers by well over their added 25% cost. In fact, organizations that have estimated the performance differential between average and top-performing employees have found that it is often 300% higher. In actuality, it is not unusual in some industries to find that the performance differential between average and top performers is 10 times (that's 1000%) higher!

Now it doesn't take a rocket scientist to realize that if you invest in an asset (whether that asset is an employee or any other financial investment) that costs 25% more but produces 1000% more in output or revenue, you have a net gain — and an outstanding one at that.

The business world is unique

The performance differential versus pay differential is extremely high in most business positions. But the same high performance-to-pay differential does not occur in all economic endeavors. In sports, for example, top performers (in the same position) are quite often paid not 25% more but as much as 10 times more than average performers. For example, Michael Jordan, in his heyday with the Bulls, was reported to be paid $35 million per season. That amount of pay was well in excess of 10 times more than the average player in his position received. Other "narrow" pay-increase-to-performance-increase ratios can be found in entertainment in the payment of movie stars.

The big secret

So why is the preceding sports example relevant? Because if top performing employees ever found out that they were dramatically "underpaid" (relative to their output), they would begin to think and act more like sports and entertainment stars. And should this "secret" get out, I am sure that top performers would rapidly get over their initial outrage and begin to demand higher pay differentials. But until they do … the lesson to be learned is that top performers are a bargain! Hire them by the dozen like a "blue light special."

What should managers do?

Lots of managers would love to hire the next Michael Jordan or Kobe Bryant of their industry, but they often shy away from even trying because they don't think they can afford them. But the evidence shows the exact opposite is true. Once managers realize that top performers are a bargain, they should demand that their recruiters and HR professionals begin to focus exclusively on hiring and retaining top performers. For CFOs, the lesson to be learned is that hiring and retaining top performers has an ROI as high as anything you can do (legally) in business … bar nothing. Top performers are cheap!

Note: Almost all business positions have an extremely high pay-to-performance ratio. But there is one major exception: that of the CEO. At the CEO level, we are all well aware of the many publicized cases where CEOs were still very highly paid (relative to other CEOs) even though they produced below-average results.

Possible Retention Metrics

Before we get to the larger universe of all employment measurements, and subsequently my own recommended "most valuable," let's take a quick look at what can be insightful with regard to retention and turnover. Great retention programs are essential to recruiting because by keeping the best people you lower your recruiting load and you avoid having a negative image as a result of having top performers "quit." In addition, the cost of losing a single top technical person can easily exceed $200,000.

Turnover and Retention Measures

The following is a list of more precise ways of measuring employee turnover. As in other metrics, the more complicated the information provided, the clearer the "story" is.

- Performance turnover: voluntary turnover rate of top 25% of a company's performers as measured by performance appraisal

- Key position turnover: voluntary turnover rate for each identified "essential/hard-to-hire" position

- Key competency turnover: voluntary turnover rate of individuals who possess skills/competencies essential to the company

- Competition turnover: % of voluntary turnover that immediately go to work for direct competitors

- Retention turnover: % of "targeted for retention" employees who leave anyway

- Exempt turnover: % of all exempt employees who leave each year

- Retention ranking by manager: ranking of managers by the voluntary turnover rates in their divisions/departments

- Benchmark turnovers: our turnover rate compared to
  - our industry average
  - our key competitor
  - last year's rate

- "Positive/good (involuntary) turnover": % of identified "low performers" (or those lacking key competencies) who leave each year

Other turnover factors
- Cost of turnover

- Business impact of turnover

- Turnover's impact on customers, image, recruiting, and the performance of other employees

The Complete Checklist of Possible Employment Metrics

After studying hundreds of employment systems at *Fortune* 500 firms, I have identified numerous metrics or measures that can be used to assess the impact and quality of employment systems. This checklist can be used as an audit tool or as a mechanism for identifying and continuously improving the employment function. Remember, effective metrics don't have to be long or complicated. Start with a long list and then get managers and financial officials to help you pare it down.

The metrics in the following long list are grouped together by their association with quality, quantity, time, customer satisfaction, or cost. The most effective metrics are those that focus on increasing revenues/performance rather than keeping costs down. Results are always more important measures than "process" measures. Data can be collected by random sampling as well as by continuous measures.

In reviewing this list, it is important to remember that all recruiting improves if:

1. Metrics related to hiring are sent to all managers on a monthly basis.

2. Managers are rewarded for great hiring.

3. Managers are trained how to do great hiring.

4. Recruiters are measured and rewarded for great hiring.

Here is the list:

Quality/Accuracy
- Performance (quality) of hires (compared to last year, your average, or industry average) in performance appraisals, forced rankings, or scores of 360-degree or team assessments

- # of "superstar" hires, in productivity rates or (reduced) error rates

- Speed of promotion of hires

- # of awards/recognitions of hires

- $ amount of bonuses/pay for performance of hires

- # or % of qualified applicants who exceed the qualifications of our best current employees

- # or % of hires who exceed the qualifications of our best current employees

- # or % of offers accepted

- % of new hires involuntary terminated

- % of unqualified applicants sent to managers

- % of diverse applicants/hires

- Accuracy of workforce demand/supply forecasts

- # or % of "agile" hires (multicapable, flexible, "continuously learning" individuals)

- # or % of top-tier (top 1%) college hires

- Accuracy of pre-employment "tests" in predicting the quality of a hire

- Accuracy of recruiters' "assessments" in predicting the quality of a hire

Quantity
- # of "offered" candidates lost to direct competitors

- # or % of all applicants who are qualified for the position

- # of total responses to our recruiting efforts

- # of recruits identified/referred per position

- % (ratio) of referred applicants who are hired (hit rate)

- % of required/scheduled employment processes (references, interviews, etc.) actually completed

- # or % of hard-to-fill positions filled

- # or % of EEO complaints/lawsuits

- # of terminations of new hires within six months of hire (voluntary and nonvoluntary)

- # or % of internal placements

- # of applicants in "applicant pool" available for "fast" hire

- % or # of "non-active" job seekers (currently employed and not looking for a job) identified

- % of recruitment sources evaluated and dropped for newer, more effective sources (per year)

- # or % of hires from our "direct" competitors

Time or Speed

- Time to respond to initial requisition (response time)

- Time until resumes received

- Time between receipt of resumes and time received by managers

- Time-to-offer/hire (time-to-fill)

- Time until termination/tenure of new hires (months of tenure rate)

- Time required for new-hire "break-in"/training

- Average # of days each position is open

- Speed-to-hire for critical/emergency positions

Customer Satisfaction (Applicants and Hiring Managers)

- % of applicants (both initial rejects and those selected for assessment) satisfied with the recruitment process

- % of hires satisfied with the recruitment process

- % of hiring managers satisfied with the recruitment process

- % of satisfied applicants for internal placements

- Ranking of employment (by managers) as a contributor to meeting their goals/profitability

- # of complaints or legal actions

- Ranking of employment by managers (as a contributor to profitability) compared to all other "overhead functions" and compared to last year's ranking

Money or Cost

- Starting salary of new hires (compared to industry average or per unit/$ of their productivity)

- $ spent on recruiting per new hire (cost per hire)

- Relocation expenses per hire

- % of total recruitment budget that is "variable" (not fixed), to allow for easy reductions during slow hire times

- % of total budget (total administrative and/or HR) spent on employment

- Lower cost per unit of employment service (e.g., per reference check) than our primary competitors'

Top 10 Recommended Employment Metrics

1. % of new hires (in key jobs) who perform at our top level by the end of the first year

2. % of new hires (in all jobs) who perform at our top level by the end of the first year

3. % of new hires (in key jobs) who perform at our lowest level by the end of the first year

4. % of new hires (in all jobs) who perform at our lowest level by the end of the first year

5. Satisfaction with the recruiting process (applicants/interviewees/new-hire satisfaction, as measured by survey)

6. Satisfaction of the hiring managers with the process and the results (as measured by survey)

7. Time to fill key jobs

8. Voluntary turnover rate of above-average performers (performance turnover)

9. Time-to-productivity (number of weeks/months until new hires meet the minimum job-performance level)

10. Response time to customer/applicant requests

11. BONUS: Track which sources provide the best-performing and highest number of hires

Characteristics of World-Class College Recruiting

No review of today's staffing metrics would be complete without a visit to the world of college recruiting. For your firm to be at the top of this game, you must make sure that:

- It hires students who perform at a significantly higher level than that of your current best employees. (Performance measurement might include new-hire productivity, sales, forced-ranking scores, performance-appraisal scores, # of raises, promotions, ideas, awards, and so forth.)

- It recognizes that hiring a significant number of college hires directly impacts the increase in profit of the firm, by increasing corporate competitiveness/capability as a result of the added capabilities provided by the new college hires.

- It understands that college recruiting programs have a higher success rate, have a greater impact on productivity, and have a higher return on investment than other recruiting systems and programs.

- It has developed an assimilation program that helps new college hires get to know the company and begin planning their careers, and helps managers and the company learn about the hires' goals and strengths.

- The quality of its college hire system allows you to attract and hire "the best and the brightest" so that "your" college recruiting system is your main competitive advantage over your main competitors.

- It is the best in The Six Primary Employment Roles:
  - Finding prospective new hires
  - Convincing them to apply
  - Selecting the most productive
  - Convincing them to accept

- Shortening their time-to-productivity
- Rapidly redeploying them to the areas where they can help the corporation the most

- Its college hire program continually innovates alternatives to existing systems.

- Its program mirrors the speed of change of its products and "obsoletes" its own "college recruiting" tools over time.

- It uses side-by-side tests, "mystery shoppers," random sampling surveys, focus groups, and pilot tests to ensure that new systems are refined (and work) before (and after) they are implemented.

- It has instant response capability for questions and problems (24 hours a day).

- Its program has a shorter cycle time, has lower unit-of-service costs, can handle a larger volume, and results in better-performing hires than the systems of direct competitors.

- Its program includes elements of product and corporate image marketing. This helps to improve the company's "image" in general, and positively impacts its ability to sell products to non-applicants and rejected applicants. The college hire program should have a reciprocal agreement with the sales staff to assist each other in finding names and selling the product.

- Its program has the capability of assisting in other strategic corporate initiatives such as mergers, acquisitions divestitures, strategic alliances, layoffs, expansion (international and national), restructuring, head count maintenance, assessment centers, and so forth.

- It identifies and assesses outsourcing and "special help" resources (event planning, career fairs, initial screening, consultants, etc.)

to handle situations where there is no advantage in having the capability internally.

- It continuously benchmarks itself against the best in the world and "audits" itself against your direct competitors. You recruit away the competitors' best recruiters.

- Its college hire program uses changing technology (e.g., WWW, intranet, video conferencing) to allow you to find, convince, and evaluate candidates in ways not possible before.

- It has JIT (just in time) capabilities to ensure you can be instantly responsive to changing business needs (e.g., instant hire, pre-grad hire, out-of-term hire).

- It minimizes the managers' time spent on administrative employment functions.

- Its college hire program continually identifies "factors" that "cause" applicants to apply. They then influence top and middle managers to provide the "best" working environment so that we can become "the" employer of choice in our industry and area.

- It has multi-approaches and customizes its strategies to the particular job or situation. It monitors the external environment and adjusts to meet the changing (job) market. It is proactive and forward-looking. It accurately forecasts future needs, college graduation rates, and the quality of future grads, and changes systems to be ready in time.

- It involves and empowers all college applicants to "own" the employment process.

- Its college hire program has as its second most important goal (after the quality of the college hire) "speed as a competitive advantage."

- It has a clear, written, and communicated college hire plan (multiyear) that is an essential element of the overall strategic business plan.

- It integrates college recruiting systems (people and computers) with other HR and "corporate" systems, to ensure cooperation and the smooth flow of information to others outside of HR. New-hire performance is tracked and success and failure data are continually "fed back" to refine recruiting and selection tools.

- It has the same or higher ethical standards than those of the rest of the industry.

- It utilizes reengineering, TQM, processes maps, pay-at-risk incentives, and other tools to continually improve.

- It develops systems to maintain security, confidentiality, and privacy.

- It uses objective and measurable decision criteria (rather than subjective or "gut" criteria) whenever possible.

- Its college recruitment department continually identifies and evaluates employment information sources (journals, reference sources, on-line sources, books, newsletters, etc.). Information is continually shared with the staff.

College Recruiting Assessment Criteria:
Should We Target a Specific School?

Use these metrics to help determine whether or how you should focus your college recruitment effort on one particular school or set of schools.

Assessment Factor

- # of qualified resumes received last year

- # of offers given in the past year

- % accepted

- Performance of hires (last two years)

- Development projects with school

- Location of school

- Ranking of school

- Number of overall applicable degree program professors, associations, projects, etc.

- Up-front costs of getting "recruiting slots" at the career center

- Relationship with key faculty

- Relationship with key student groups

- # of alumni at our firm who are willing to help in our recruitment efforts

- Degree of recruiting competition at the school

- Size of the student body in applicable majors

- Curriculum related to specific needs

- Potential to influence curriculum

- Success at influencing students to take a co-op/internship

- Potential for strategic relationship

- External recommendations

- Internal recommendations

- Current relationship with school

- Sales to school

- Potential of sales to school

Thoughts on the Future of Staffing

Recruiters are often too busy finding candidates and "closing deals" to spend much of their time worrying about the future of their profession. Recruiters, independent agencies, and executive search firms have a big surprise in store for them if they are not aware of how the changing world of business will soon impact them.

In the 21st century, it will no longer be possible to survive using traditional tools.

Recruiters tend to be the type of people who "learn by doing. Unfortunately, the old ways of "doing" recruitment are rapidly becoming obsolete, so recruiters need to develop new ways to learn about the changing world of recruitment and business. They need to be aware of a number of areas, including globalization, technology, and the growing number of "work at home" jobs.

The U.S. is leading the way in this change effort, and U.S. firms are already well on their way toward obsolescing many of the traditional recruiting practices we are accustomed to using. This next generation of recruiting will be both exciting and challenging for those who are prepared — and threatening to those who are not.

The process of recruiting has changed dramatically in the last few years. Web pages, electronic resume scanning, e-mail, and other innovations have forever changed the way we look for candidates. The employment process will continue to change, and will rely more and more on technology due to:

- The growth of "easy to use" technology, cheap at-home PCs, and the increasing willingness of candidates and recruiters to use them.

- The globalization of firms and worldwide worker shortages, which mean that recruiters must now search the globe for candidates.

- The growth of "remote" and at-home work, which will make looking for jobs less and less tied to firms located within a commuting distance from home.

- The continuing shift away from physical labor toward knowledge workers who are more willing to search for a job on the Web.

- The decline in newspaper subscriptions (and their want ads as recruiting tools).

Additional factors contributing to the change in the recruitment paradigm are vacillating unemployment rates, and the expectation of long-term employment with a single firm becoming the exception rather than the rule. As a result, there will be a dramatic increase in the number of times in our lifetime that we will be in the job-search mode.

For recruiters, this means more work.

For individuals, it means that great job-search skills will become a lifelong necessity — not just something that they will just occasionally need!

The next chapter will shift from recruiting to training and professional development. Metrics are especially important here because training is often one of the first HR functions to the cut when times are tough.

Chapter Three
Training Metrics

3

Goal of this chapter

The purpose of this chapter is to highlight some of the criticisms that training receives and then to provide you with a variety of tools and metrics that will help you build your credibility among managers and employees.

As a function, training often comes under fire when talk turns to performance, because little has been done to prove that providing training demonstrates a positive business impact, and therefore a substantial return on investment. Unfortunately, this means that when budgets get tighter, training is one of the first areas within an organization to get cut.

Training's Trouble Spots: Why It's One of the First Things to Get Cut When Dollars Are Tight

However, lack of demonstrated performance isn't the only reason metrics need to be applied to training. The following are just a few of the things managers have had to say about training that can all be countered or proven true with the right metrics:

- Managers don't believe that training provides a "value-add" for top performers, and some think that it can actually harm the firm by pulling them away from their work.

- Training has little data to show what percentage of performance improvement normally occurs on an individual basis after they go through a training program. This causes managers to ask, What is the justification for doing it?

- Many of my employees state that they could learn more effectively using a training tool of their own choosing.

- Training as a function is so isolated from the others that it almost appears to be completely separate.

- There are no direct compensation rewards for successfully completing training or for managers who keep their employees well trained.

- Training does little to help assess employees, or to ensure that a team has all the skills it will need in the near future.

- Rarely does training follow up to see how successful a program was, other than to ask if people "liked it."

- Training has never demonstrated a clear process for proving cause and effect, or for proving that a program will actually solve the organization's problem.

With those points under consideration, you probably already have a few training measurements in mind. But prior to developing some metrics to counter the above problems, you should think about some of the goals for using metrics in training. Your goals should be a good mix of ones that are internally focused and ones that are externally focused. Just responding to the above statements will give you a good start toward establishing some external goals, but the following list should help you balance them out.

Goals for World-Class Training Metrics

Internal

- To help secure additional funds for the training budget

- To keep the training budget from being cut dramatically during tough times

- To self-identify areas in need of improvement with current training programs

- To demonstrate your results-oriented focus to senior managers

- To identify what budget allocation mix will contribute the most to the organization

External/Business Impact

- To identify what capabilities will be needed by the organization in the future, and that are currently in short supply

- To determine what inventory of skills is needed to provide us with a competitive advantage in our industry

- To demonstrate training's impact on increasing productivity

- To provide marketing data (on the amount and quality of training available) for use by staffing in attracting top performers

- To provide a demonstrated impact on the retention of key employees

- To increase the quality and speed of management decisions, time-to-market. and product development

A Checklist of Metrics for Measuring Training Effectiveness and Impact

Training can be measured in a variety of ways, ranging from recording simple stated interest to more thorough methods that evaluate changes in performance. Here are five levels of training effectiveness measures, with the metrics of each listed in increasing order of business value.

A. Prior to Training

1. % of the target population who say they need it during a needs assessment process.

2. Corresponding number of people who actually sign up for and attend it.

B. At the End of the Training

1. The number of people who attend the specific session.

2. The number of people who paid or would be willing to pay to attend the session.

3. Customer satisfaction of attendees at the end of the training session.

4. Customer satisfaction at end of training, when customers know the actual costs of the training.

5. A measurable change in knowledge or skill at end of training (testing).

6. Ability to solve a "mock" problem at end of training (testing).

7. % stating willingness to try or intent to use the skill/knowledge at end of training.

C. Delayed Impact (Non-Job)

1. Customer satisfaction at X weeks after the end of training.

2. Customer satisfaction at X weeks after the training, when customers know the actual costs of the training.

3. Retention of knowledge X weeks after the end of training (testing).

4. Ability to solve a "mock" problem at X weeks after end of training (testing).

5. % stating willingness to try or intent to use the skill/knowledge X weeks after the end of the training session.

D. On-the-Job Behavior Change

1. % of trained individuals who self-report that they changed their behavior/used the skill or knowledge on the job after the training (within X months).

2. % of trained individuals whose managers report that they changed their behavior/used the skill or knowledge on the job after the training (within X months).

3. % of trained individuals who actually are observed to have changed their behavior/use the skill or knowledge on the job after the training (within X months).

E. On-the-Job Performance Change

1. % of trained individuals who self-report that their actual job performance changed as a result of their changed behavior/skill (within X months).

2. % of trained individuals whose managers report that their actual job performance changed as a result of their changed behavior/skill (within X months).

3. # of trained individuals whose managers report that their job performance changed (as a result of their changed behavior/skill), either through improved performance-appraisal scores or specific notations about the training on the performance-appraisal form (within X months).

4. % of trained individuals who have observable/measurable (improved sales, quality, speed, etc.) improvement in their actual job performance as a result of their changed behavior/skill (within X months).

5. The performance change of the total employee population who are managed by (or are part of the same team as) individuals who went through the training.

6. Departmental performance change in departments with X% of employees who went through training.

7. ROI (cost/benefit ratio of return) on training dollar spent (compared to our competition, last year, other offered training, preset goals, etc.).

Other Miscellaneous Measures

1. CEO/top management knowledge of/approval of/satisfaction with the training program.

2. Rank of training seminar in forced ranking by managers of what factors (among miscellaneous staff functions) contributed most to productivity/profitability improvement.

3. # or % of referrals to the training by those who have previously attended the training.

4. Additional # of people who were trained (cross-trained) by those who have previously attended the training, and their change in skill/behavior/performance.

5. Popularity (attendance or ranking) of the program compared to others (for voluntary training programs).

6. % of total HR costs allocated to training.

7. % of training available on-line.

8. Cycle time (months) in developing new training programs.

9. Cost per participant.

10. % of employees participating in voluntary training.

11. % of training programs taught by line managers.

After you select the basic set of metrics you will use to assess your training function you might want to consider raising the bar and assessing whether your organization is a learning organization. Those metrics are included in the next section.

Building the Business Case —
Questions Training Professionals Should Be Able to Answer

The following is a list of metrics and suggestions on how to improve training. They are put in the form of questions that heads of training can ask themselves when they are assessing their training programs.

- Are managers measured and rewarded for the development of their employees?

- Are employees rewarded for continuous learning and development?

- When you ask top performers the key to their success, in forced ranking where does training fall?

- When you ask top performers how they stay on the bleeding edge, do they cite training?

- What is the percentage of employees who have individual challenge, growth, and/or learning plans?

- If surveyed, what rank would training receive in an annual survey of managers (on how they perceive the different overhead functions that have contributed to their productivity)?

- How is training rated on employee satisfaction surveys and on 360-degree assessments?

- How often is lack of training is cited as a reason for leaving a firm?

- Do people cite our training as why they applied/accepted our offers?

- Does a large change in the amount spent on training (a significant increase or decrease) have a similar impact on output?

- Can we show that training can increase the performance of an average performer to that of a top performer?

- Why are there no if-then and what-if training scenarios to help managers prepare for upcoming events?

- Do we know that training changes behavior?

- Have split samples been used to measure the impact of specific training programs?

- Why not make the EE own their own training and give them a % of their salary that is devoted to professional development?

Assessing Your Training Organization —
Is Your Organization a Learning Organization?

If your organization currently measures training using advanced metrics, then there is a good chance your organization is a learning organization. A learning organization is one that truly values the personal and professional growth of its employees, and that has developed robust systems to ensure that training needs are effectively being met and that rewards are in place for doing so. While many organizations would consider themselves learning organizations, few actually are.

To see how your firm stacks up, run your organization through the following assessment. If you can agree with 15 of the following 20 statements, then your organization can be considered a learning organization.

Measuring a Learning Organization

Many people consider becoming a "learning organization" to be the ultimate goal of any manager of training and development. Utilize this checklist to see where you are on your path to this goal.

1. Managers routinely discuss and champion effective training and development programs with other managers within the organization. The new training programs are requested by managers.

2. The percentage of new product and process ideas that come from the bottom 30% of the organization is greater than the percentage of new ideas that come from the top 30%.

3. Employees are actively involved in gathering data about the industry and our competitors, which is leveraged by the training organization to assist in developing a competitive advantage.

4. The percentage of our employees who are continuous self-learners is greater than that of those who require formal training classes in order to improve.

5. Formal systems are in place to enable all employees to share ideas and information about events within the industry that directly relate to our competitive advantage.

6. Training tools are provided that enable employees to "learn fast" and "on the run/on the job."

7. More than 75% of corporate information is available through self-service on the company's intranet.

8. The percentage of the total budget that is dedicated to professional development expressed as a % of an individual's salary is at least 110% of the industry average.

9. Our managers are directly measured and rewarded for the development and improvement of their employees.

10. Employees are rewarded for continuous learning and development.

11. More than 80% of the employees have individual challenge, growth, and/or learning plans.

12. "Learning metrics" are kept corporate-wide and are part of top management's year-end metrics.

13. The firm does continuous competitive intelligence gathering to determine how fast and accurate their training research is.

14. The ranking that training receives in the annual survey of managers (on how they see that the different overhead functions have contributed to their productivity) places training in the top five.

15. Employees have an opportunity to rate the effectiveness of their training on employee satisfaction surveys and on 360-degree performance assessments.

16. Lack of training is cited as a reason for leaving a firm less than 5% of the time.

17. New hires rate training as one of the top five reasons why they accepted their job.

18. The time it takes for a new skill or policy to take hold in the organization following training is measured and is demonstrating a decreasing trend.

19. More than 50% of all new training programs allow for self-service or remote training.

20. Competitors copy or benchmark your training programs … instead of you copying theirs.

21. Your training programs are ranked (given awards) by national journals/organizations.

22. Training is mentioned in the annual report and in the CEO's speeches.

23. The training budget exceeds 5 percent of total payroll.

Questions from the CEO!

With information gathered from metrics explained in this chapter (and the remainder of the book in general), you should easily be able to handle the following questions from your CEO. In fact, you should be hoping that these questions are asked.

- Does having well-trained employees really make a difference in our industry?

- Are our people the most productive in the industry? Does training impact productivity?

- Does pay/hiring/ER/retention increase employee output more than training?

- Does training actually improve our people — make them more skilled and productive?

- Does having a well-funded training function help us attract and retain the very best people?

- Does training work fast enough to make a difference?

- Is there evidence that training is a major contributor (among overhead functions) to our corporate success/profitability?

- Do we forecast and prevent training problems better than the best in the industry?

- Is our training department efficient, and does it continually improve?

- Are our managers/employees "satisfied" with our training function?

- Do we rapidly redeploy our training resources from low-return areas to high-return ones?

- Do we define our overall training strategy and align it with our business strategy?

- Is there evidence that training adds significantly to our shareholders' value?

- Does training work for all? Or is it better in key jobs? Or for certain people?

- If I doubled your budget ... would productivity double?

- Do our senior managers cite training as a key factor in their development and promotions?

Concluding Thoughts on Training

Firms frequently waste training dollars on low-impact, ineffectual programs that have little lasting impact on customer satisfaction, cost containment, or quality improvement. Many training programs operate on "blind faith." They assume that they are having a positive business impact. As new electronic training possibilities evolve, pressure will be put on training functions to cut expenses and most classroom training. The challenge now is to develop new approaches and programs that will be available on an employee's desktop.

Too often, companies rely on theory lectures, inspirational speeches, videos, discussion groups, and simulation exercises to provide their message. While these methods may get satisfactory marks from participants, research shows that they rarely change behavior on the job.

Failing to link training with organizational strategies and day-to-day management behavior also wastes training dollars. Trainees learn which hoops to jump through, pledge alliance to the current management fad, give their enthusiastic "commitment to building the new culture" — and then go back to work. Why? Because training is offering help that lags behind or that fails to mesh with the overall business strategy.

Here are a few points to consider:

- Effective training builds how-to skills that are highly relevant and immediately applicable. A study by one firm showed that trainees retained a paltry 13% of skills six months after training if managers failed to provide coaching and support as the skills were being applied.

- It's important to build training around organizational objectives and strategies. Trainees should immediately see the connection between their new skills and where the organization is going. This makes training more relevant and gets everyone focused on applying his or her new skills to the organization's key priorities and goals.

- Have the CEO and other senior managers deliver sessions personally to the organization. This trend of "cascading" training down from senior management snaps everyone to attention. Training attendance problems disappear. Trainees don't cross their arms and ask, "Is the organization really serious about this stuff?" In addition, managers achieve a deeper level of skill development when they teach others, and are put on the spot to practice what they are now preaching.

In the next chapter, you will find multiple ways to assess and measure compensation.

Chapter Four
Compensation Metrics

4

Goals of this chapter

If compensation is to move beyond its role as a basic overhead function, it must increase its business impact. That shift will require an increased use of metrics, and new strategies that use compensation and nonmonetary incentives to directly increase motivation, productivity, and innovation.

Compensation Is a Strategic Function

Strategic functions are those that:

- Impact all departments

- Affect product development and customer satisfaction

- Significantly impact profitability

Compensation fits each of these three criteria. But not all compensation functions act strategically. If you want to understand the impact compensation can have on a company, consider the following points.

If your company has a turnover rate of 20% per year as a result of poor compensation, then compensation can impact the business. If, in addition, all of your replacement hires are mediocre performers because your pay system does not attract the best applicants, it will take only five years for your entire workforce to be unmotivated, and that is a strategic problem.

If you don't pay people correctly, they can work as much as 15% below their capabilities. Great ideas and products come from motivated people — not from disgruntled employees, equipment, buildings, or capital.

The cost of "bad" pay practices must include decreased product development. For example, if a lead software engineer on a product development team works at 80% of their capability, the cost to a company over a year can exceed millions of dollars because it slows time-to-market. Competitors who might not otherwise have beaten you to the market may now do so, capturing the valuable first-mover advantage.

No one purposely pays people incorrectly, but weak compensation efforts will negatively impact productivity, retention, hiring, and time-to-market.

The Business Impacts of Having Weak Incentive Programs (That Result in Unmotivated Employees)

When you pay people incorrectly, you demotivate them. As a result, you increase the potential for a variety of productivity-impacting things to happen. Each of the impacts specified below suggests a variety of metrics that can and should be monitored by compensation.

Increased Management Time and Effort
- Unmotivated employees require "high maintenance" and more management attention.

- Time spent on "problem" unmotivated employees can't be spent on the best employees, thereby creating a scenario where top performers are neglected/punished.

- Unmotivated management and team leader positions have a multiplier effect on the productivity of others.

Training Time and Costs
- Unmotivated employees, because they often fail to maintain their competencies, require more training than actively engaged employees who learn on the job and through dialogue with others.

- The time unmotivated employees spend in training slows their "time-to-productivity."

Customer Satisfaction and Error Rates
- Unmotivated employees send a message to our customers that we are getting weak or that we don't care about them.

- Errors and perceived "bad attitudes" by unmotivated employees cost us sales volume and occasionally customers.

Product Development

- Unmotivated employees offer fewer ideas — and mediocre ideas at best, when they do, which distract us from where we really need to be going.

- Time-to-market is dramatically impacted by the disruption caused by their mediocre ideas and questions, and because they do not fit well into a team of motivated "winners."

- Trying to humor them or not hurt their feelings when they don't understand what the rest of the team is trying to do wastes time and energy. We answer their questions and politely try to help them come up to speed, when this help wouldn't be necessary if they "got it."

Our Competitive Advantage

- A unmotivated employee takes up a spot on the team that can't be taken by a superstar. These are called opportunity costs!

- Unmotivated employees produce less per dollar of cost (salary), and their "complaining" demotivates others. Since typically 60% of all corporate budgets go to employee expenses, that makes the inefficient use of these funds a major corporate weakness.

- Unmotivated CEOs and top managers can adversely impact our stock price and the willingness of others to partner/merge with (or invest in) us.

Other Employees' Productivity

- Superstar employees often resent being on the same team with "unmotivated losers."

- Team productivity can suffer due to time lost in helping the weaker, unmotivated employee.

Our Image and PR

- Unmotivated employees send a message to future recruits that we are not concerned about motivating employees.

- Unmotivated employees send a message to our current employees that we are headed downhill.

Proving That Great Compensation Works

What compensation needs to do is to prove, using metrics, that great compensation practices affect a firm's ability to develop a great workforce that:

- Possesses more competencies than the average, both competencies that we need now and will need in the future.

- Is agile, and can multitask and shift rapidly to new problems and jobs.

- Self-develops, and is composed of continuously learning individuals who learn without the need for company training.

- Has more ideas that are implemented and that impact our profitability.

- Requires "low maintenance" from managers, because of lower error rates, and decreased disciplinary incidents and absenteeism rates.

- Produces higher customer satisfaction, and has higher performance-appraisal scores, bonus rates, forced-ranking scores, and promotion rates.

- Inspires and trains others to be more productive.

- Stays longer before quitting.

- Produces more return for every dollar of salary paid them.

It's that simple.

Unmotivated employees cost us a bundle, and motivated ones make us rich!

What Makes Up World-Class Compensation?

This checklist is designed to help you determine whether your best efforts are world-class. These criteria, although detailed and sometimes cumbersome, are necessary because of the magnitude of their impact on the success of both individuals and the firm itself.

World-class compensation programs differ significantly from average compensation efforts. Not all programs strive to be world-class, but those that do meet most of the following criteria.

World-Class Compensation Programs:

- Maintain at least a 25% differential in the rewards between top performers and average performers

- Have a measurable business impact (profit, productivity, time-to-market, customer satisfaction, etc.)

- Have as a goal differentiation in rewards, not equity

- Have a positive return on investment and a short payback period

- Are agile, and can shift their focus as motivation and retention needs change

- Utilize the latest technology to improve the quality of the compensation program

- Provide and measure quality service (even to remote locations)

- Have top management and employee buy-in

- Have multiple measurable goals that are prioritized or weighted, and meet each of them

- Have programs and incentives that encourage teamwork and cooperative efforts, as opposed to encouraging functional "silos" and independent action

- Are seamless to the customer. An employee or manager who has a problem in compensation can get an answer with "one stop shopping"

- Are based on sound motivation theory, and the compensation department can prove why they work

- Encourage the attraction and retention of high-potential/high-performing individuals

- Increase the corporate image (as a company that pays and rewards well) as an employer of choice

- Reward "good" behaviors, tell managers and employees what is important, and energize actions

- Improve the performance of marginal workers

- Rapidly redeploy compensation resources from areas of low return to areas of high return

- Are benchmarked against the best compensation practices of leading firms

- Fit the corporate culture, mission, and values

- Anticipate potential internal problems (in compensation and motivation), and have options to avoid or minimize each

- Have compensation program costs (per unit of service) below those of competitors

- Are more effective than the competitors'. If our company pays in the 75th percentile, then our productivity and retention rates should also be in the 75th percentile (or above) within the industry

- Have compensation mentioned by new hires as one of the top five reasons for joining the firm

- Have compensation mentioned during exit interviews as a prime reason for leaving in less than 10% of the cases

Metrics for Assessing Compensation Program Impact

What should you measure in compensation? Here is a list of some advanced questions (with action steps) that you should be able to answer.

People profit. What are your average people compensation costs (salary and benefits and compensation function costs) per dollar of profit? Show the trend over several years (and project future years), and compare it to your chief competitors'.

People revenue. What are your average people compensation costs (salary and benefits and compensation function costs) per dollar of revenue? Show the trend over several years (and project future years), and compare it to your chief competitors'.

Impact of pay increases. What % of increase in employee output (or performance-appraisal scores, or retention rates) results from every 1% increase in pay? Show the trend over several years (and project future years), and compare it to your chief competitors'.

Pay quartile impact. Do the employees paid in the top quartile of the salary range produce proportionally more output (PA scores) than those paid in the bottom quartile?

Impact of highly paid people. After completing a benchmark study of your industry, do a correlation analysis to see if the firms that pay their employees at the top of the range are more profitable than those that pay at the middle or bottom of the range.

Dollar of output per dollar of people costs. What is your productivity (dollar value of the product/service produced) per dollar of people compensation costs (salary and benefits and compensation function costs)? Show the trend over several years (and project future years), and compare it to your chief competitors'.

Forced ranking and pay. If a forced ranking is used, do all those with top rankings get paid at a level equivalent to their ranking?

Compensation Department operational expenses. What % of total corporate expenses are Compensation Department operational costs? Show the trend and compare it to your chief competitors'.

Increase in total compensation costs. Show that the percentage of total pay/benefits costs to total corporate costs stays the same or goes *down* over time.

Impact on human capital. What impact have compensation practices had on increasing the value of your firm's human capital (the value of ideas, knowledge, etc.)? What is that value? Show the trend and compare it to your chief competitors'.

Impact on corporate change. What has compensation done to increase your rate of corporate change and continuous improvement? How has compensation helped in attracting, retaining, and developing top talent? Show the trend and compare it to your chief competitors'. Show that compensation has helped make your firm the employer of choice in your industry.

Under-/overpaying? Demonstrate that you have a system for identifying and forecasting whether you are under- or overpaying your employees.

Maximize pay-at-risk. Demonstrate that you have closely tied the maximum amount of all employees' compensation to increases in productivity and company performance. Show the difference in productivity of "high" pay-at-risk divisions versus no or low pay-at-risk divisions. Show that every year your employees produce more for every dollar of salary and benefits paid.

Compensation forecasts (strategic planning and forecasting). Demonstrate that you are providing the CEO and the board with accurate and timely information, advice, and forecasts on the future compensation needs of the corporation.

Executive compensation. Demonstrate that the Compensation Department is providing the board with accurate information on executive and BOD pay and performance-assessment tools. Demonstrate how the execution of the strategic compensation plan over the last "X" years has contributed to your overall bottom line, stock price/market value, and/or overall competitiveness. Show the business impact that the compensation function has had, as demonstrated in your company's annual reports.

Contribution to profitability. Conduct a survey among line managers and ask them to do a "forced ranking" of all administrative functions (compensation, employment, accounting, MIS, etc.), to show which function contributed to/helped them the most to increase profitability. Assess overall customer satisfaction with the responsiveness of compensation services, and show that it improves each year.

Corporate capabilities and competitiveness. Can you demonstrate that "superior" human talent is a sustainable competitive advantage (sometimes also known as an industry "critical success factor") that will allow those with the best talent to crush the competition? Can you show that superior compensation practices directly impact your ability to attract, retain, and motivate superior talent? Will the value of human talent increase in the future? Will the value of excellent compensation practices increase in the future?

Rate of continuous improvement. Demonstrate how you have continuously improved the output of the compensation function at (at least) the same rate the company must improve its products. Show how your compensation function is superior to your competitors'.

Questions from the CEO!

Once again: After using the metrics pointed out in this chapter, you should be able to easily answer these questions from your CEO.

- Does compensation really matter in achieving faster, cheaper, and better business results?

- Do we spend more or less than our competitors in total compensation (TC) in order to get the same results (e.g., sales, unit of production, profit)?

- Does increasing the pay of an individual have any impact on the employee's performance/productivity?

- What percentage of total corporate expenditures is attributed to pay/benefits costs? Has that ratio stayed the same, or does it go down over time?

- Can compensation managers demonstrate that we have a system for identifying and forecasting whether we are under- or overpaying individual employees?

- Can we demonstrate the impact of placing employees' pay at risk based on output and performance, as opposed to the same amount as base pay?

- Can we show that we have closely tied the maximum amount of all employees' compensation directly to increases in productivity and company performance?

- Does compensation ever forecast future trends in order to give managers heads-up advice on what future salary demands will likely be?

- Which compensation tool has the most impact on productivity? If nonmonetary tools have a large impact, why doesn't the Compensation Department have specialists in nonmonetary compensation?

Concluding Thoughts on Compensation and Benefits

Great compensation programs should increase productivity, but sometimes there is a disconnect!

For example, let's look at possible disconnects in the area of benefits.

Goal: Reward for performance.
Disconnect: Health benefits are the same for all, with no change in payments based on performance.

Goal: Rewards vary with position impact.
Disconnect: A key project leader gets the same benefits as the janitor.

Goal: Reward levels change with company profitability.
Disconnect: Vacation leave doesn't vary with company profitability/productivity.

Goal: Penalty for increasing expenses.
Disconnect: Having more children and having a spouse increase medical benefits but not productivity. Single people get "less" no matter how productive they are.

Goal: Reinforce company culture.
Disconnect: Vacation allocations are based on the number of years of service, not performance.

Goal: Prove that benefit programs work.
Disconnect: We pay for education expenses, but we do not reward people when they complete a program, and we have no data to show that performance increases as a result of completing the education.

As difficult as it may be, it's important to eliminate such disconnects, and align compensation with productivity!

Compensation principles
- Reward people differently, based on actual performance. There should be no rewards for "just showing up."

- Positions with the most impact should have a greater opportunity for reward than low-impact positions.

- Reward levels should vary up and down when the overall performance (profitability) of the company changes.

- Behaviors that increase a company's expenses but don't increase productivity should have a penalty attached.

- All compensation programs should reinforce — not contradict — the corporate culture and values.

The next chapter covers metrics related to performance management and employee relations.

Chapter Five

Metrics for Employee Relations

5

The goal of this chapter

Managing people on a daily basis is a complex task that is made even more difficult because most employee relations professionals are averse to using metrics. The use of measures and metrics can help employee relations managers to identify trends and patterns. This chapter outlines several different ways to measure the effectiveness of the employee relations and performance management functions.

In any company, it is wise to frequently measure the effectiveness of the employee relations function and its processes. This is done to prevent or detect an ongoing systemic problem within the company. It can also lessen the probability of lawsuits and decreased productivity due to localized employee issues.

As a function, employee relations focuses on something critical to the success of any organization: individual performance. Through periodic performance assessments and emergency response programs, world-class employee relations' specialists can dramatically impact a firm's bottom line.

Characteristics of a World-Class Employee Relations (ER) System

What follows is a list of 41 characteristics that a world-class employee relations system should demonstrate. You can utilize this checklist for assessing whether you have a world-class ER system. Not all of these factors can be applied to all firms and all cases, but the more statements you can agree to regarding your system, the better.

1. Our employees are the most productive in the industry and are more productive than they were last year, comparing output per dollar compensated.

2. Our ER system forecasts and prevents ER problems.

3. Following an internal disturbance, our employees return to productivity more quickly than those of our competitors.

4. Our system frequently (quarterly) provides objective performance measurement (appraisal) using methods all parties involved validate as accurate and fair.

5. A complete set of ER metrics is prepared and distributed to all managers routinely.

6. All policies are clear, tested, and communicated. There is proof that the policies actually change behavior.

7. Employees and managers are involved, so they "co-own" people problems.

8. Managers are rewarded for excellent performance in ER matters.

9. Climate or attitude surveys are done frequently to measure the organization's "pulse."

10. Past practice and ER cases are well documented.

11. All ER systems are paperless and are available on a manager's desktop

12. All ER processes are cost-effective (while maintaining quality).

13. More ER time is spent on top performers than on low performers.

14. ER has maintained a union-free environment or a partner relationship with the union.

15. Our ER system follows due process/just cause.

16. ER trains all managers in dealing with ER issues directly, and how to spot warning signs.

17. Our system has a credible appeal/review process (in the eyes of employees).

18. There is on-line ER training and access to FAQs.

19. Fair investigations occur without delay.

20. All punishments fit the crime.

21. Successful (winning) lawyers assess all major cases for errors and risk assessment.

23. Employees have 24/7 access to their personnel files (which are electronic).

24. Our system never "assumes" facts — it finds out for sure.

25. Our system maintains employee dignity.

26. Our system seeks legal assistance when appropriate, but doesn't let lawyers "run the show."

27. ER judgments are based on business necessity and ROI.

28. Our system uses "mystery shoppers" to test ER systems.

29. Our system considers alternatives to firing when appropriate.

30. We keep employee issues private and available only on a "need to know" basis.

31. Our system has global capability (and flexibility).

32. Our system involves employees in preventing ER problems.

33. We expect a low turnover of top performers and a high turnover of low performers.

34. Our ER processes contribute to a higher morale level (this year when compared to last year).

35. Our system achieves respect and support from managers.

36. We turn OK performers into great ones.

37. We win over 70% of the cases we take to court.

38. We use technology wherever possible.

39. We use "expert" systems to improve and decentralize management ER decision-making.

40. Our system proves cause and effect where possible, and identifies "why" incidents occurred.

41. Our system improves the performance of workers it "works with" by at least 20%.

Metrics for Assessing ER Program Impact

ER metrics in this section are broken down by each of the key metric elements.

Quantity

- \# of complaints filed per employee per period of time
- % of cases settled without progressing to court/arbitration
- % of cases resolved with NO monetary settlement
- \# and % of turnover attributed to ER conflicts
- Number of big-payoff cases, e.g., sexual harassment, discrimination, etc.
- % of employees who are aware of our ER policies and rules (indicating that they are clearly communicated, understood, and documented)
- % of cases lost due to poor documentation
- % of employees who feel that their privacy is protected
- % of employees who feel that the punishment fits the crime
- \# of actions taken as a result of exit interviews

Time

- Response time when there is a complaint to an ER specialist
- Conduct investigations promptly
- Hours of ER training taken by managers
- % of management time spent on ER issues

Money

- Cost of an average complaint
- % of payroll spent on ER costs

Payouts for lawsuits

- Cost of lawyers

- # of hours ($) in management time spent on ER issues

Quality

- Amount of negative publicity

- % of employees rating their morale as high

- Turnover rate of top performers

- Turnover rate of bottom performers

- % of bottom performers that become top performers

Conclusion

Most employee relations departments judge their success by subjective "process" measures. A better approach is to assess overall employee improvement and productivity.

This section completes the coverage of the different individual HR function. The next chapter covers metrics for assessing and improving the effectiveness of the overall HR function.

Chapter Six
Metrics for the Entire HR Organization

6

Goals of this chapter

Now that we have looked at metrics for most major HR functions, it's time to take a step back and look at the big picture. How can you improve the effectiveness of the overall HR function and what role can metrics and service-level agreements play in that improvement process? Most of the metrics outlined in this chapter are designed for use by the top manager of a particular function. But even if you're not a senior manager, you might get an idea of what they look for when they measure the effectiveness of a program or function.

HR and Organizational Effectiveness: It's All About the Bottom Line

The major things that HR can really do to impact a firm are in the areas of:

- Attraction of talent

- Retention of talent

- Productivity management

- Time-to-market capability

- Innovation

Outside of these five key areas, HR is involved mainly in procedural and administrative types of activities that will never add significant value regardless of the efficiency and economy with which they are executed. In order to build a truly world-class HR function — and rise above the status of business partner to that of business *leader* — HR must focus metrics more on organizational (the firm's) effectiveness than on internal improvement.

Other executives, including the CEO and CFO — who often has control of the HR budget — are more interested in metrics that demonstrate what impact various HR strategies and actions have had on the business versus metrics that show how functional efficiency increased or decreased. Unfortunately, most organizations currently using metrics in HR seldom make a clear connection between HR efforts and key business.

Here are the basic HR metrics that you need to use if you are going to demonstrate your business impact.

Develop an HR Dashboard, Index, Internal Improvement Monitors, and "Smoke Detectors"

You can't improve what you don't measure, so metrics are a crucial element of great HR. I recommend that you utilize each of the four basic categories of HR metrics.

The four categories of HR metrics:

1. The first is a "dashboard" (like a car dashboard), which is so named because it allows you to continually monitor all of the vital elements in a successful HR function.

2. The second approach is an HR "index," which is a single combined index that allows you to see how you are doing at a single glance, very much like the Dow Jones average gives you a quick glance of how the stock market is doing.

3. The third is individual self-improvement metrics used for efficiency improvement. Not all metrics are strategic. Some minor ones should be monitored for no other reason than to ensure that the function can continue to improve at a regular rate.

4. The final approach is developing "alerts" or warning metrics (called smoke detectors). Their role is to provide managers with sufficient advance warning of upcoming potential problems

Examples of the four basic categories of HR measures, the HR dashboard metrics, an HR index, HR internal improvement metrics, and smoke detectors are found in the next sections.

1) HR dashboard

The Dashboard Approach — Putting Metrics Where You Can See Them
A measurement dashboard consists of a combination of metrics indicators that are continually monitored to identify problems and predict potential future problems and issues. Think of it as the instrument cluster of an advanced race car that provides real-time feedback on the functional performance of all critical systems in the car. If your organization is technology-savvy, such dashboards can be implemented across the organization via a Web-based front end. A simplified dashboard example follows at the end of this section.

A dashboard to help continually monitor HR performance on a daily basis
The following are items which might be monitored on a daily basis by a senior HR manager. The concept is simple: View each of the different measures on a regular basis and identify any better trending towards the negative. You use the dashboard to identify potential opportunities or trouble areas within the overall HR function.

Here are some examples of metrics that can be part of a "dashboard":

High-level metrics

Overall labor costs per unit of output (remember, 60% of all organizational costs are EE costs)

- Increase in profit/revenue per $ spent on people

- % of manager satisfaction

- Accuracy of workforce forecasts

- % of HR goals that were met

- Average % of improvement in each functional HR program

- Senior management's forced ranking of HR as a contributor to organizational results (as compared to other overhead functions)

- Employee pulse/satisfaction. What are the employees saying?

- Success in becoming an employer of choice or improving our recruiting image

- Quarterly human assets review and overall HR performance index

Recruiting

- Performance of new hires (determined via forced ranking, rating, bonus)

- Time-to-fill — Average delay in filling a position (target hire date versus actual hire date)

- Manager satisfaction with the hiring process

- Applicant satisfaction with the hiring process

- Offer acceptance/rejection rate

- Number of unfilled positions

Training/Education

- Average training hours per employee

- Participant satisfaction with training

- % of new hires who give training opportunities as a Top 5 reason for accepting

- % of employees who cite a lack of training as a Top 5 reason for leaving

- % of employees who list a lack of quality training as a Top 5 inhibitor of their productivity

- % of managers who cite training and education as a roadblock to time-to-market, innovation, and productivity

Compensation

- Percentage of employees' pay above/below the target market

- % of new hires who give our excellent total compensation approach as a Top 5 reason for accepting

- % of employees who cite a weak compensation approach as a Top 5 reason for leaving

- % of employees who list a weak compensation approach as a Top 5 inhibitor to their productivity

- % of overall pay that is at risk (tied to performance and stock price)

- Change in the ratio of dollar spent in comp benefits and total revenue

- % of managers who cite comp benefits as a roadblock to time-to-market, innovation, and productivity

- % of all managers' pay that is tied to great people management

Employee Relations

- Turnover rate of top performers/people in key jobs

- Turnover rate of bottom performers

- % of employees who are satisfied with our people practices in our employee pulse survey

- % of managers who cite ER as a roadblock to time-to-market, innovation, and productivity

- % of employees who feel challenged, growing, and recognized by their manager (for retention purposes)

- % of direct managers rated as weak in pulse and 360-degree assessments

- % of employees and managers noted as "needs improvement" who left the firm

- Dollar costs defending legal issues and suits

- % of diversity goals that have been met

HRIS

- Percentage of HR transactions that are paperless

- % of HR managers satisfied with HRIS's contribution to overall HR improvement

- % of frequently asked HR questions and transactions that can be (easily) handled on the Web through self-service

Example of a staffing dashboard

Staffing Dashboard

Metric	Last Year	3-Month	3-Month Running Average	Current	Warning Level
New-Hire Performance (based on performance-appraisal scores at 6 months)	3.4	3.6	3.78	3.65	3.5
Cost-per-Hire (Dollars)	5,800	4,250	4,400	4,700	5,000
Time-to-Fill (Days)	61	37	33	31	30
Time-to-Fill Key Positions (Days)	37	26	21	19	20
Time-to-Productivity (elapsed time from date of hire to time when minimum output achieved)	45	42	44	43	45
% of Hires from Referrals	32	36	38	41	40
% of Hires from Web	35	37	34	32	50
Turnover Rate of Top Performers	6.8	4.7	4.9	5.1	3

Metrics that appear in bold in the "Current" column are currently below acceptable minimum performance, indicating that immediate attention is required.

2) Overall HR Indexes — For Judging Performance "At a Glance"

The HR Index — A Thermometer for HR/Functional Health

When analysts talk about the health of a company, or the health of the economy, they rarely talk of change in a specific measure of performance, but rather a combined set of measures referred to in statistical terms as an index.

In the business world, indexes are all around us; two of the most well known are the Dow Jones Industrial Average and the NASDAQ Index. Each of these indexes provides insight into the health of the capital markets they represent by combining movements of all of the securities they deal in into a single metric that can at a glance indicate what the entire market is doing on average: going up or going down.

An HR Index works along the same principles, combining changes of several measures that relate to the performance of the HR function as a whole, or one of its functional units, into a single metric that indicates function health.

Here is an example of an Overall HR Index; an index for the staffing function is opposite. The metrics included are those recommended by me; however, you may certainly adjust them to reflect your own organization's indicator prefer-

Overall HR Index

Weight of factor	HR factor to be included in the index
20%	Revenue (or profit) per employee
15%	Turnover of top/bottom performers
15%	Performance of recent hires
15%	% of key employees' pay at risk
10%	% of EEs satisfied with the Big 6
10%	Turnover rate of poor managers
5%	Manager satisfaction with HR
5%	Time to fill key jobs
5%	Diversity ratios of the workforce

This sample index of overall HR performance includes nine different weighted factors

ences. *Remember that HR metrics — like stock prices — have both positive and negative connotations attached to upward and downward movements, so attention to detail should be paid to ensure that your index adequately reflects a true summarized performance.*

Functional Index (A comprehensive single index for an individual function as an indicator of overall employment function "health")
Here's an example of an index that can be used to monitor the relative "health" or state of an HR function. Although the function in this case is staffing, the concept works for every HR function. If you need to compare employment performance between this month's and last's or between divisions, a single index is the best approach. An employment index is the averaged score of several weighted employment measures. It is a simple measure of employment "health," and it's easy to track on a single chart.

Staffing Function Health

Measure	Weight	Current	Norm	Variance	Positive Value	Actual Value	Weighted Variance
New-Hire Performance	25%	3.2	4.0	20%	+	-	(5%)
Percent of Hires from EE Referral	20%	50%	40%	25%	+	+	5%
Time-to-Fill	15%	36 Days	30 Days	20%	-	+	(3%)
Screen-to-Interview Lag Time	15%	4 Days	5 Days	20%	-	-	3%
Manager Satisfaction with Staffing Organization	15%	79.2%	90%	12%	+	-	(1.8%)
Exempt Diversity Hiring Ratio	10%	14%	10%	40%	+	+	4%
						Variance Subtotal	2.2%
						100 Basis Points	100.0%
						Total Weighted Performance	102.2%

To create a health index for a team, department, or function, a selection of metrics is pulled together and weighted according to their level of importance to the team's or department's success. Targets, also known as "norm values," are established for each metric. To determine the health of the team or department, actual performance values are compared to the norm values and combined to create a single score that is representative of the overall group's health. The steps are outlined below:

Step	Activity
1	Select a grouping of metrics that measures the group's performance against its core deliverables.
2	Weight each metric according to its relative importance to group success.
3	Determine a target value or "norm value" for each metric. This is the base performance level at which the group will be considered to have met expectations.
4	For each metric, determine whether an actual performance value that is greater than the norm value is a positive or negative thing. If it is positive, place a "+" in the column labeled "Positive Value" If it is negative, place a "-" in the column.
5	Collect the actual performance values for each of the metrics in your index.
6	Divide the actual performance value by the norm value for each of your metrics.
7	Subtract the result from 1.0, and record the result in the "Variance" column.
8	Multiply the variance for each metric by the metrics "Weight," then again by 100. Record the result in the column labeled "Weighted Variance."
9	If the "Positive Value" and "Actual Value" contain the same symbol, then the weighted variance should be a positive value. If the two columns do not contain the same symbol, the variance should be expressed as a negative.
10	Sum the variance values for the index, and place the result in the "Subtotal" cell.
11	Add 100 basis points to the Subtotal, and record the result in the cell labeled "Total Weighted Performance."

A total weighted performance value of 100 means that the group whose health is being measured is performing at the current level of expectations. A value of less than 100 means that the group is performing below expectations, while a score above 100 indicates above-average expectations performance.

3) HR Internal (Self-) Improvement Metrics

After utilizing the first two categories of metrics (HR dashboard and HR index) the next category to be considered is internal improvement metrics. Most of these are not significant enough to be reported outside of HR, but each can be helpful in defining and improving the overall efficiency of HR. Some call them minor metrics, but I disagree. They are important but only to an internal audience of HR managers.

Some Internal Improvement HR Metrics to Consider

There are some metrics that can give insight into what and why things are happening in an organization. Using them might improve your overall perspective on what's happening.

List of possible internal HR metrics:

- HR customer satisfaction data (courtesy and quality of service)

- HR budget utilization

- Response time to requests for HR help/information

- Cost-per-unit of HR service (this year compared to last)

- HRIS-related performance and customer-service metrics

- Number of internal transfers

- Salary grade distributions

- Span of control statistics

- Performance appraisals on time (without a quality-of-PA metric)

- % or # of vacant HR positions

- Turnover rate within HR

- List of critical terminations and open positions

- List of high-performing employees who are at risk of leaving

- Competency "gaps" between needed and actual organizational capabilities

- Degree of self-service available to managers

- Number of relocations processed

- Number of expatriates processed, and their satisfaction

- "Usage or utilization" of HR services by department or program

- % of HR services shifted to self-service or to managers

- % of globalization of services available internationally and 24 hours a day

Often-Used Internal HR Metrics That Can Be Improved

- Head count by itself is misleading — because not all positions pay the same. Dollars spent on employees, as a percent of revenue, is a better metric if costs are the issue.

- Turnover is misleading — if it doesn't show the importance of the person leaving. Turnover in key positions and high-performance-rating turnover is more revealing.

- Hidden costs. The "real costs" are not universally used in many HR reports. For example, there is often no cost listed for losing an employee, but there is a cost listed for hiring one.

- Offer rejects by job or division, in addition to the overall numbers, can help HR target problem areas.

Alerts, Smoke Detectors and Warnings:
Using Metrics to Warn You of Potential Danger

Often in life, we get caught up in day-to-day activities and fail to keep a broad perspective that might warn us of upcoming danger. To remedy this and to help prevent surprises, many systems present in our lives today have developed warning mechanisms.

One of the most common is the smoke detector or alert. A smoke detector provides all of those within range of its horn a warning that a potential catastrophic emergency exists, and that action is needed immediately. While sometimes these sirens do end in non-emergency situations, in the cases when an actual emergency does exist, they provide enough warning to possibly solve the problem before total loss is imminent.

The same concept can be utilized within HR to warn of potential people emergencies, by developing metrics programs that have a consistent monitoring element. Employee relations events like employee turnover almost always have "precursors" (predictors) that, if tracked, can give you advanced warning of soon-to-occur events.

The sources of data that would drive such a program often readily exist, yet even most large business units on the cutting edge have failed to make connections to external events (like unemployment rates, changes in market share, competitor actions, etc.) that directly impact their operations. A planned strategy that includes data- and information-gathering can provide managers with sufficient lead time so that they can successfully avoid or minimize any large-scale problems in their business unit.

Using turnover as an example problem, let's look at the following as possible smoke detectors to indicate that a potential problem might exist:

- A significant decrease in productivity/production

- An increased number of applications for internal transfers

- An increased number of "sudden retirements"

- An increased turnover rate among your high-performers

- A decrease in 360-degree or satisfaction survey ratings

- An increased volume of rampant rumors

- A dramatic increase in the volume of internal e-mail in the employee chat room

- Increased "open door" visits

- A dramatic decrease in applications, Web site hits, or offer acceptance rates

- Rumors or occurrence of recent significant events like layoffs, stock price drops, change in top management

- Increasingly negative returns from "coffee talks," focus groups, and simply asking employees if they are unhappy

- A sudden increase in absenteeism or employee tardiness

- An increased refusal of overtime

- The unemployment rates drops below 4%

Although smoke detectors might seem difficult to develop, many HR professionals and seasoned managers already can "sense" upcoming problems. What is needed is a more formalized approach that can aid all managers (not just those with internal sensors). Start with a simple approach using only a few measures, and refine it over time. Keep in mind that nothing impresses managers more than accurate predictions. If you warn them just once about a superstar employee who might leave (in time to prevent it), you will have instant credibility for your next warning.

Additional Suggestions for Improving HR Metrics

Improving the HR function and elevating it to a leadership position will require that every aspect of HR become performance-oriented. To ensure that your metrics aid in this process, keep the following suggestions in mind for how to improve your metrics efforts.

1. Metric use must be universal — Using metrics is a primary step in developing a "performance culture." HR metrics need to be specified for each HR function or program. Just because metrics are difficult for some in HR is no excuse to exempt a program from utilizing them. Metrics use must become a way of life. Also remember to measure and report "informal" HR programs that are often overlooked because they were never "formally" designed or proposed.

2. Metrics require targets — If the goal is to improve all HR programs and services, then performance targets for each program need to be set in advance. Performance targets are the actual numerical goals or expectations each program is expected to meet. The differential or gaps between the expected and the actual need to be reported frequently to all (yes, embarrassment has some motivational value).

3. You must compare — There needs to be a competitive analysis (a side-by-side comparison) of the performance metrics of direct product and talent competitors. In addition, compare internal performance trends with the use of multiyear analysis and averages. A side-by-side comparison makes the assessment of continuous improvement much easier.

4. Improve metrics as new data becomes available — As the amount and quality of data available improves (as companies automate more functions), metrics need to be revisited and improved.

5. Ask customers — The process for adding and dropping metrics needs to be tied into a customer survey. Make sure you know what metrics actually help managers make decisions and which ones don't provide much value. Metrics can be improved if there is an R&D aspect of HR to examine the adding and dropping of HR metrics.

6. Don't exempt the generalist — Many HR departments use "generalist" in many of their business functions. Unfortunately, many generalists resist the "watchful eye" of metrics. If generalists are in use, then metrics need to be maintained for each generalist and in each activity area.

7. Program improvement rates — One of the most effective ways to manage HR programs is to monitor the percentage that they improve in performance each year. As a result, the speed of HR program improvement/obsolescence needs to be tracked, reported, and compared.

8. Changing the organization — Since the ultimate goal of HR is to change the organization and the behaviors of individuals, it is also important for HR to attempt to monitor how HR has increased the organization's (business) capabilities and learning speed.

9. Fee-for-service — If you believe in market forces (as most business managers do), HR should monitor which programs are good enough to cause managers to agree to pay a fee-for-service for them. Without a doubt, the best way to find out if your service is valuable is to have managers pay directly for it with cash.

10. Use "mystery shoppers" — Don't assume that things are going well or that answers are accurate. The use of random sampling with "testers" to assess the actual quality and accuracy of HR advice, service, and information is an important quality check mechanism.

Advanced Measures for Assessing HR's Real Business Impact — What Your CEO Wants to Know About HR

Most HR measurements miss the boat because they are mostly tactical measurements. Most of the metrics done by HR are disappointing to most CEOs and CFOs. Although many HR departments say that they are a "business partner," few can provide any real evidence that they are having a strategic business impact. After years of studying CEO expectations of HR, I've compiled a list of the kinds of questions CEOs might want answered about how their "human resources" give them a measurable competitive advantage over their competitors.

If you're really knowledgeable in HR, try answering the following questions. And if you can, then run your answers by the CEO to gauge his or her reaction.

1. Does having great employees and HR really make a difference in our industry?

    *   Does HR have evidence that having "the best" employees is a Critical Success Factor (CSF) in our industry, because the most profitable firms have a high proportion of "quality" employees and the less successful firms have a lower proportion of "quality" ones?
    *   Has HR identified the jobs or functional areas where having great people is essential for corporate success (a CSF)?
    *   Does adding more HR resources (budget) make a difference? Is the return on investment in HR higher than the ROI on capital or for plant and equipment?
    *   Do the best firms in our industry have great HR departments, and do the mediocre-performing ones have mediocre HR? Does improving the HR department impact a firm's competitive position?

2. Are the people we have the MOST PRODUCTIVE in the industry?

   - What is our firm's productivity (output) per dollar of people costs spent? (People costs include: salary, benefits, training, and HR Dept. costs.) Can HR show the trend (over several years and project future years) and compare it to our chief competitors'?
   - What is our "people profit" (the number of dollars of "people" costs we must incur in order to generate a dollar of profit)? What is the trend, and how does it compare to our chief competitors' numbers?
   - What is our "revenue per employee"? Is it higher than our competitors'?

3. Do we have the RIGHT NUMBER OF PEOPLE in our organization?

   - Does HR have a metric/system for ensuring that we are not OVERSTAFFED? Do we compare our head count per unit of production/sales to that of our direct competitors to ensure that we don't have head count "fat"?
   - Are we UNDERSTAFFED in areas? If we added people in key areas, would we increase our profitability?

4. Are we OVERPAYING our employees for the output they produce?

   - Can HR show the impact of pay increases? What is the % increase in employee performance as the result of every 1% increase in pay?
   - Does paying top dollar matter? Do the employees paid in the top quartile of the salary range produce proportionally more output than those paid in the middle quartile?
   - Demonstrate that we have tied a higher proportion of our total compensation to productivity and company

performance than our competitors. How much differently do we treat (pay) our top contributors than our average contributors?

- Whom are we over-/underpaying? Demonstrate that we have an effective system for identifying and forecasting whether we are under- or overpaying our employees.
- Is there evidence that our benefits programs really attract or keep people?

5. Do we IMPROVE the people we have (make them more skilled and productive)?

- Is having good training a Critical Success Factor in our industry? Is there a correlation in our industry between the % of all people costs spent on training/OD and firm profitability?
- Does training make a difference in performance? What is the % increase in performance as a result of every $1,000 spent on training?
- Training also needs to prove it is closing the gap between current competencies and needed future competencies at our firm.

6. Do we attract and HIRE the very best people we can afford?

- Did we hire better people this year (more productive per dollar spent in salary) than last?
- Demonstrate that we are hiring people with competencies and skills that give us a competitive advantage over our competitors.
- When we compete head-to-head with our competitors for top-tier talent, show that we get a higher percentage than our competitors.
- Show that you have made our firm the employer of choice in our industry.

7. Do we RETAIN our key/most productive people at a higher rate than our best competitors?

   - Show that our voluntary turnover rate is lower than our competitors for:
     - Key executives
     - Top performers
     - Individuals with "key" competencies
     - All individuals in hard-to-hire positions

8. Do we "FIX" OUR "PROBLEM" EMPLOYEES rapidly or get rid of them if they are too expensive to "fix"?

   - What percentage of "poor" performers become "very good" performers within a year, as a result of our employee relations efforts?
   - Show that we get rid of our poor performers who can't be "fixed" at a rate faster than our competitors'.
   - Is there evidence that HR identifies and effectively "fixes" "bad" managers?

9. Is there evidence that HR provides guidance and help to STRENGTHEN our managers and teams? Is it a major contributor (among overhead functions) to our corporate success/profitability?

   - Do we survey our managers and ask them to force-rank all overhead functions on how they contributed to departmental and divisional profitability? Does HR rank toward the top?
   - Does HR provide evidence that it contributes to increasing our shared vision and the strengthening of our corporate culture?
   - In our employee pulse survey, do employees rate HR as a contributor or a barrier to productivity?
   - Does HR give managers multi-options, and do its programs allow managers to "adjust" corporate policies to fit "local"

needs? We give managers input into policies before they are initiated.

- Do we sell management on the importance of people issues? We educate managers and teams on the HR implications of actions they take (or might take). Do we make a compelling case to managers that people issues should get the most time and attention?
- We give managers options on the "level of service" they receive from HR.

10. Do we FORECAST and PREVENT PEOPLE PROBLEMS better than the best in the industry?

- Have HR's "smoke detectors" and forecasts given top management sufficient warning of possible "people problems"? Have they allowed us to effectively mitigate the impact of "people problems" upon the business?
- Programs and solutions are developed by HR before smoke turns into fire, and before managers have to request them.
- Do we provide our managers with sufficient lead time and a "heads up" on people issues that they will face?

11. Is our HR department efficient and does it CONTINUALLY IMPROVE?

- Is there evidence that HR continually improves its programs? Drops its ineffective ones?
- Is there evidence that putting more HR resources in an area dramatically impacts that area's productivity and profitability?
- What percent of all corporate spending goes to HR? How does it compare to last year and our best competitors' percents? Are our costs per unit of HR service below those of our best competitors, given an equal quality of service?

- Do key departments and products get the most Human Resources help?

12. Are our employees "SATISFIED"?

- Do employees report that they are more satisfied this year with the way they are treated, compared to last year?
- Does HR have evidence of the impact of employee satisfaction on our employees' productivity and retention?

13. Do we rapidly REDEPLOY our people resources from areas of low return in the corporation to areas of high return?

- What % of our workforce moves internally each year between business units?
- What % of our workforce have we had to lay off this year?
- Is there evidence that we get the most from our talent?

14. Is our overall HR STRATEGY ALIGNED with our business strategy?

- What is our overall HR strategy?
- Is there evidence that it adequately shifts as our business needs change?
- Has HR done a competitive analysis (overall and by function) to see where we need to shift our efforts in order to beat our competitors in every HR category?
- Does our HR strategy reinforce our corporate values and culture?

15. Is there evidence that HR has significantly ADDED TO OUR SHAREHOLDERS' VALUE?

- Has our stock options program added to or diluted our shares' value?
- Because, on average, over 60% of all corporate dollars are spent on people costs, demonstrate what HR has done to

increase our overall corporate capabilities, competencies, and capacity to beat our competitors.

How did you do? Yes, these are not easy questions to answer, but remember that merely saying that HR is strategic is no longer sufficient. In a tough business world, you must be able to prove it. However, if you can answer each of the above questions, you are more than strategic ... you are an HR hero!

Steps in Becoming a Strategic HR Department/Program

Developing great HR Metrics is only one part of becoming strategic within HR. In addition to metrics, there are the steps you need to take in order to become strategic. Some of the essential elements of a strategic HR Department include:

HR should focus on the future — That means you must anticipate the future and know where the industry, the competitors, and the general business environment are headed.

- Be knowledgeable about the firm — It's important to know the company's business plan and what new products and services it is planning to offer. You can't be a business partner or leader unless you know the business as well as the managers who use your services.

- Reduce cycle time — In a world that moves incredibly fast, HR can't be the speed-of-change laggard. Aim to improve your "speed" until you are the fastest-responding and -adapting overhead unit in the firm.

- Lead with technology — In a world dominated by technology, HR can't afford to be labeled as the "Stone Age" department. Utilize company intranets and internal Web sites for core administration whenever possible — both for speed, cost savings, and for improving your image.

- Measure and reward people performance — Managers won't take great people management seriously until it is measured, reported, and rewarded.

- Help in gaining competitive advantage — Your firm's products must compete directly with those of the competitors. If you expect HR to be great, you must offer HR program performance that is superior in each area to that of the direct competitor. Do continual competitive intelligence and side-by-side comparisons to build and maintain your lead.

- Focus on business impact — HR programs don't live in isolation. If your programs don't improve the cooperation and success of the business … you are a failure. Always measure actual business impact when developing a new program, to ensure that it has a business impact outside the HR function.

- Have the capacity to continually learn fast — In a world where what you know loses value by the hour, the primary competitive advantage becomes learning speed. If everyone in HR isn't on the "bleeding edge" of knowledge, you can never become world-class.

- Prioritize HR services — Not all business units or positions have equal value to the firm. Once you realize that, you must build a strategic decision framework that allows the department to shift and focus resources on key business-impact areas.

Advanced Steps in Becoming Strategic

In addition to the strategic steps that were just outlined, there are some additional things you can do, including:

HR Goals

- Increasing "people productivity" and reducing labor costs should be business impact goals (and metrics).

- Setting "best-in-class" service as a goal provides a major competitive advantage.

- HR must identify and then manage to the critical success factors in the industry. You must find out what separates the winner from the "also-rans" in people management.

- All HR dollars must be measured based on return on investment.

- Reacting is not enough. HR must forecast and anticipate problems. A future focus must be maintained, and you must develop systems to predict future needs.

- The overall goal for HR needs to be faster, better, cheaper, continuously improving in everything you do. Great HR realizes that it must … obsolete itself!

Reward Everything That Matters

- Measures, reporting and rewards are "the" most effective motivators

- Identify key performance indicators (KPI) and reward them all, including:
    - Short-term performance
    - Long-term performance
    - Individual performance
    - Line-of-sight team performance
    - Out-of-sight team (division/corporate) performance

Tie HR Rewards to the Business-Unit Performance

- Business results are all that matter. Overhead function rewards (including HR) need to be tied to business-level performance. So if the ship sinks, we all go under.

Customer Satisfaction

- Employee satisfaction is an end goal. You must assume that employee satisfaction causes customer satisfaction.

- Managers are your customers. First, educate managers about what is possible — but then give them what they say they want, even if occasionally it's basic handholding.

Don't Confuse Having Programs and "Effort" With Success

- Many HR departments confuse implementing "programs" with actual business impact. Some go further and assume that good, sincere, hardworking people (in HR) automatically produce results. Never confuse effort with results.

If you need additional tips on becoming strategic in HR, visit my Web site at www.drjohnsullivan.com.

Concluding Thoughts on Strategic HR

I am admittedly a critic of the way most people look at HR strategy and practice. In this final section, I have highlighted an area in each major HR function that needs reconsideration.

- Recruiting — Great employment is recruiting QUALITY people who produce more per dollar of salary paid. Track the productivity of hires after they are hired to see if the ones you hire become top performers.

- Training — In training, it is the change in productivity as a result of training programs that really matters. If training does not change performance … drop it.

- Compensation — Compensation should work to get the pay (and benefits, as much as possible) of all employees directly tied to productivity. There should be no "showing up" rewards. If at least 20% of employee pay is not tied to performance, you will never be able to attract or retain top performers. In addition, individual managers should set all the pay of their employees and be accountable for the productivity and profitability (per dollar spent on pay and benefits) they get.

- Employee relations — ER specialists and consultants should improve the productivity of the workers they deal with. Fix them in X months or get rid of them. Most HR functions spend too much time on bottom performers, and they have little evidence to show that the "bottom" performers ever improve. Poor-performer turnover needs to be 100%. And HR should be proactive (working with employment and managers) in reducing the voluntary turnover of high-performers to less than 3%.

- HR technology — HRIS is more complex. Responsiveness and customer satisfaction should be heavily incented. HRIS should have specific performance goals related to speed, error rate, and cost per transaction. Paperless HR, resume scanning, and HR metrics are a minimal requirement.

- If you can only do one overall metric, use productivity per dollar of employee and HR expense. Option B is profit per dollar of employee and HR expense. These ratios need to be contrasted "this year's to last year's," and to those of our closest competitors. In case of doubt, ask your CFO what impresses them in terms of numbers and metrics. If they do not buy it, no one else will, either.

- HR can be a profit center — In my experience, HR is a profit center. We spend over 60% (on average) of ALL corporate dollars on people-related expenses. There needs to be a higher ROI on people expenditures than from finance, MIS, and production programs if we are to be *business leaders*.

Chapter Seven

Getting and Using the Right Data for Your Metrics

After you decide what metrics to use, without a doubt the next greatest roadblock to getting any world-class metrics program/effort started is finding or collecting the data. Here, data means just the numbers and the quantified results or outputs of programs. Unfortunately, while HR as an organization is often thought of as the keeper of all employee-related data, the truth is that much of the information collected historically by HR is in a form that has little value when it comes to metrics. The key reason for this is consistency — or, better put, inconsistency.

For any metrics effort to provide valid insight, the components used to make up those metrics must also each to be valid.

Within HR, many programs and processes have been developed on an ad hoc basis, meaning that in many cases little thought has gone into gathering and producing usable data. Since our processes and procedures were not designed to produce data that could be used in more than one place, the data archived by them is often in the wrong format, or it is broken out into units that make analysis of it difficult.

With that said, you must commit early-on to the idea that issues relating to past program design will not derail your efforts to implement metrics. When processes are identified that do not produce reusable outputs (data), then in some cases they must be at least tweaked so that the captured data exists in a form that is reusable.

Finding Existing Data: It's All Around You

Existing data is all around us, but when pressed to locate it, many of us often leave out many potential sources. As a result, we often settle for the most easily accessible data, even when such data isn't exactly what we need. However, don't despair. Conversations with financial, IT, or production managers often reveal that more "existing" data is available than you initially thought.

Sources for Data

There are two categories of sources for data: internal and external. Internal data is information gathered within the company, and external data is information gathered from external sources. Gathering internal data used to be the easiest of the two, but with the growth of the Internet, collecting external data has in many cases become much easier. In the following sections you will find listings identifying the different types of sources that most HR departments use for data collection. Note that because most HR professionals have a limited amount of time to spend, the sources are broken into existing and newly created sources of data.

External Sources of Existing Data

External data are defined as information gathered outside the corporation. Generally, the external information you need comes from industry sources, government agencies, and consulting firms. The types of information you might need for your metrics from already existing sources include economic data, industry data, and benchmark data on functional performance. Some HR examples are included (within the parentheses) in the following list.

1. Functional association's benchmark reports (SHRM, the World of Work, COEB, and IHRIM)

2. Benchmarking association studies (the Conference Board, Corporate Leadership Council, the American Productivity and Quality Council)

3. Industry associations

4. Consulting firms

5. Data from other firms' efforts (obtained directly from the firm)

6. Periodicals (*HR* Magazine, *HR Executive*, *Training* Magazine, and *IHRIM Journal*)

7. Academic research (especially from Cornell, the University of Michigan, and the University of Minnesota)

8. Reference books

9. Government agencies (reports, studies, databases; Departments of Labor and Commerce)

10. Vendors and suppliers (HRIS, staffing, and training vendors)

11. HR benchmark organizations — (the Saratoga Institute and staffing.org)

12. Web sites (SHRM, Workforce, Staffing.org)

Internal Sources of Existing Data

Some typical internal sources of data include:

1. Corporate financial reports (federal filings, annual reports, etc.)

2. Past employee satisfaction/opinion surveys

3. 360-degree assessment data

4. Output/production reports

5. Marketing collateral

6. Sales forecasts

7. Budgets

8. Exit interviews

9. Orientation surveys

10. Payroll and benefits information

11. Performance appraisals

12. Employee files

13. Audits

14. Customer surveys

15. Data previously collected via corporate forms (comment cards, employee documents, sales agreements, etc.). Keep in mind that other functions collect data, too. Ask around: Someone else may already collect what you need.

16. ERP and other functional software

17. Your company intranet

External Sources of New Data

When customized new external data is required, most HR professionals turn to consulting firms. There are external firms that will do "just in time" surveys of both current and ex-employees as well as specialized benchmark studies and competitive analysis.

1. Consulting firm studies

2. Opinion surveys, focus groups, and interviews conducted by research firms

3. Self-commissioned benchmark studies

5. Self-funded academic research by an intern, grad student, or faculty member

6. A consortium of firms with similar needs

Internal Sources of New Data

When customized new internal data is required, most HR professionals turn to:

1. Joint research with another function (finance, marketing, etc.)

2. New financial data

3. Surveys, focus groups, interviews (done by recruiting, employee relations or the OD function)

4. Data generated by new software

The Best Tools for Collecting the Best Data

As a consultant and professor, I constantly deal with efforts by others to collect data. I am continuously amazed by the number of people who do not understand data collection jargon. There are only two key things to differentiate between:

- Tools for collecting information
- Tools for clarifying, categorizing, or making data consistent

When people are asked how they intend to collect data, the overwhelming response is either "interview others" or "conduct a survey."

Common tools for collecting information in HR are:

- Interviews
- Surveys
- Focus groups
- Observation
- Mechanical or electronic counters
- Forms or questionnaires (on-line or paper)

Tools for Clarifying, Categorizing or Making Data Consistent

To make tools for collecting information more useful, there needs to be some underlying process that is designed to yield consistent data. If we were interviewing candidates for a top position, and we had a number of potential hires, then it would make sense to evaluate them using a consistent method — e.g., asking the same questions of each, running the same simulations, and so forth. What follows are several tools/methods to help the above-mentioned collection tools yield more consistent data.

Forced ranking

This tool is one with which many are familiar, and one that many employees have grown to question in progressive organizations that use it in their performance-appraisal process. Forced ranking asks the participant to order a set of values from those most important or critical to those less important or least critical. In the case of performance appraisals, forced

---

Forced Ranking Example

Directions: Use the following form to rank potential changes to our corporate Paid Time Off (PTO) Program. Of the five potential changes, number them according to your preference, from 1 to 5, 1 being the most desirable to you, 5 being the least. When you are done every list item should have a distinct number next to it, i.e. no two list items can have the same rank.

Rank   **Proposed Change**

PTO hours earned in the current year, but not used by year end may be cashed out during the final pay period of the fiscal year.

_____

PTO hours earned in the current year, but not used by year end may be rolled over into the following year, up to a maximum of 200 hours.

_____

The accrual rate for PTO will change to 1 hour for every week of service for employees with 1-3 years of consecutive service, and 2 hours for every week of service for employees with 4 or more years of consecutive service.

_____

Employees opting to work on all recognized holidays at a managers request will accrue PTO at a rate of 3 times that of their standard accrual rate for each holiday worked.

_____

Employees who have returned to employment following a separation from the company may accrue benefits as if all terms of service have been consecutive.

_____

ranking would ask a manager to provide an ordered list that places employees according to their importance or contribution made toward meeting the group's objectives. This tool is most often used when the list of arguments to be measured is limited in size. Forced ranking makes easier comparisons both within and between business units.

Likert scales

This tool is also one known by many, even though the name may seem foreign. Likert scales ask participants to identify to what degree they agree or disagree with a specific statement. Normally, participants are given a range of three to five options, ranging from strongly agree to strongly disagree, with a neutral option in the center.

Likert Scaling Example

Directions: Use the following form to rate comments made about your working environment. For each comment fill in only one bubble, corresponding to the degree to which you agree/disagree with the comment as written. If the comment does not relate to you, or you simple do not have an oppinion, please fill in the bubble corresponding to "Neither Agree Nor Disagree."

	Strongly Agree	Agree	Neither Agree Nor Disagree	Disagree	Strongly Disagree
1. I feel I get along well with my peers.	O	O	O	O	O
2. I am proud of the way I have handled conflict on the job.	O	O	O	O	O
3. I feel confident that I can talk to my manager about issues that arise	O	O	O	O	O
4. I am aware that my peers respect me.	O	O	O	O	O
5. I feel that I contribute value on a daily basis.	O	O	O	O	O
6. I feel good about what I do.	O	O	O	O	O

Scaling

As a tool, this one is similar to the Likert scale. However, in this case, participants rank a statement along a scale of one to five or ten. This tool is very helpful when the number of arguments to be measured is greater than five.

Scaling Example

Directions: Use the following form to score potential changes to our corporate Paid Time Off (PTO) Program. Of the five potential changes, score each on a scale of 0 to 10, 0 being highly undesirable, 10 being highly desirable. When you are done every list item should have a score next to it. You may assign the same score to multiple list items if you desire those items equally.

Score   **Proposed Change**

_____
PTO hours earned in the current year, but not used by year end may be cashed out during the final pay period of the fiscal year.

_____
PTO hours earned in the current year, but not used by year end may be rolled over into the following year, up to a maximum of 200 hours.

_____
The accrual rate for PTO will change to 1 hour for every week of service for employees with 1-3 years of consecutive service, and 2 hours for every week of service for employees with 4 or more years of consecutive service.

_____
Employees opting to work on all recognized holidays at a managers request will accrue PTO at a rate of 3 times that of their standard accrual rate for each holiday worked.

_____
Employees who have returned to employment following a separation from the company may accrue benefits as if all terms of service have been consecutive.

Weighting

The weighting method of assigning measures proves very useful when you are trying to ascertain the relative importance or significance an individual assigns to a limited number of variables, such as components of a total pay package. Via this tool, participants split or distribute 100 points across a range of potential options, assigning a greater weight to those options that have a greater relative importance.

Some organizations have begun using this tool prior to making an offer of employment as a means to identify the expectations of potential employees. The tool is very useful in helping to ensure that you meet the expec-

---

Weighting Example

Directions: The following form asks you to allocate 100 percentage points across a range of options. For each of the employment offer components listed below, allocate a percentage of the 100 points possible to demonstrate the relative value of that offer component to you in making a decision. Multiple components can be weighted identically, but the sum of all point allocations must not exceed 100. Assign the greatest number of points to the component that most influences your decision, and the smallest number of points to the component that least influences your decision.

_____ Base Compensation	_____ Manager
_____ Benefits	_____ Work Location
_____ Stock Options	_____ Type of Work
_____ ESOP	_____ Training Opportunities
_____ Vacation Plan	_____ Co-workers
_____ Bonus Potential	_____ Growth Potential

tations of a customer prior to delivery, because it enables you to adjust the expectations of the other party when you know you may not be able to meet them. This is often called aligning expectations.

Duplicate questions

If you need to improve your confidence in any one answer you can ask the "same" (or reworded) question again later in the interview or survey. This acts as a double check by making sure that the same answer is provided the second time around.

Anonymity

If you want honesty, you sometimes must guarantee that the person answering has their identity protected. In sensitive areas, this can improve the person's willingness to provide negative information.

Semantic Differentials

This final tool is perhaps the most difficult to use, but also one of the most powerful. It presents participants with a series of extreme opposite statements, such as high quality and low quality, separated by a point scale normally incorporating five or seven points. Participants are asked to identify where along the scale an organization, program, or individual fits into

---

Semantic Differential Example

Directions: Below please find a list of attributes that could be used to define your manager. On the left hand side you will find one attribute, on the right hand side the direct opposite, Use the range of bubbles appearing between each pair to score where your manager would rate with regards to each pair. Select only one bubble per pair of attributes.

Respectful	O O O O O O O	Disrespectful
Attentive	O O O O O O O	Inconsiderate
Responsible	O O O O O O O	Irresponsible
Friendly	O O O O O O O	Unfriendly
Fair	O O O O O O O	Unfair
Honest	O O O O O O O	Dishonest
Capable	O O O O O O O	Incapable
Humble	O O O O O O O	Arrogant

---

the two opposites — e.g., is the object more technology-friendly or technology-illiterate? Responses across a pool of participants are then averaged and presented graphically, comparing your organization or program to an ideal/target or competitor-offered program. The tool can also be used without comparison to force individuals to make trade-offs between program offerings — e.g., would you lean more toward quality or capacity? Toward cash compensation or equity?

Defining data "quality" needs

To ensure that we use the most appropriate data, you must define in advance the three most important elements of data:

- Quality needed. What degree of accuracy is required from the data source?

- Time frame. How much time do we have to collect and analyze the data?

- Money/cost. How much do we have to spend on getting/analyzing the data?

When you meet with managers in your search for data, be sure to specify the quality, when you need it, and how much should be spent gathering it.

Final thoughts on data collection

If you happen to be lucky and work at a high-tech firm, you are likely to find all the high-quality data that you need — without spending much time or money. In other organizations gathering data can be more difficult, but the secret is persistence. Many departments within a company collect a great deal of data, but they are often reluctant to let others know out of fear that others will "force" them to gather more or different data. The key to success in building relationships is going slowly. Start identifying data availability long before you finalize your metrics. Your best allies are often senior managers or financial professionals who support any departmental efforts to use metrics to improve efficiency. My experience has been that, overall, there is more data available than you need. The real difficulty lies in getting people to admit that they have it.

Chapter Eight

Impressing Managers — Making a "Business Case" and Using Service-Level Agreements

One of the most significant problems facing HR is credibility. During tight economic times, almost invariably, HR budgets are cut back. But even during good times, HR professionals often have a difficult time in getting new programs funded or approved. The best way to build credibility with senior managers and financial professionals is by providing a good economic or business case. A business case is an argument, using primarily numbers, which highlights the economic benefit of HR program to the company. A second underutilized tool for convincing managers of HR's competence is a service-level agreement. A service-level agreement is a formalized promise to provide a certain quality and level of HR services to a business unit. Utilized together, they both provide a powerful mechanism to build credible relationships with managers. Both of these tools are outlined in this chapter.

Making the Business Case for HR: A Step-by-Step Guide

Human Resource functions have always undergone intense scrutiny by executives and financial officers. Although CEOs are notorious for saying that people are their most important asset, they often become relative "misers" when it comes to funding people programs. If HR professionals are to survive and prosper, it is essential that they refocus their efforts on "building the business case" for investing in human capital programs.

A business case is not an output of a metrics program, but rather something in which metrics play a major role. Building a business case is really just about "selling with numbers." Most financial professionals and executives are very logical people. What they expect is surprisingly consistent in all different sizes of businesses.

What follows are the steps you must take in order to build an effective business case. While you are going through these steps, it is important to step back occasionally and view the "big picture."

You are trying to sell an idea, just as a salesperson sells his or her product. In order to be successful, you must focus on the decision-making criteria that your target audience uses. Be aware that the decision criteria listed below are, by their very nature, generic. If you want to maximize your effectiveness, you need to do your own internal research in order to identify the specific decision criteria and the "passing scores" that are utilized within your own organization.

The Elements of an Effective HR Business Case

1. Identify whom you are trying to influence.

Although we live in a world of computers, most "buy or don't buy" decisions are made by real people. Even though they might serve as a team or work together as a unit, each individual has their own set of decision criteria that they use to determine if a project is fundable. You can't treat all of the decision-makers the same and you probably don't have time to influence them all, so you must prioritize them and focus on those individual decision-makers who have the most "influence" on program decisions. "Knowing" these people and how they make decisions is not only the first step, but also the most important one in building a business case.

- Identify and prioritize your target audience. Identify which people are most influential. Also, identify any strong individuals who frequently serve as gatekeepers or who frequently exercise "veto" power over proposed programs. Next, prioritize the target audience and focus your efforts on the most influential ones. When possible, try to get one of the most influential individuals to "sponsor" the program. If you can convince an executive known as an "HR program-hater" to sponsor it, the game is already halfway over.

- Identify their decision criteria. After reviewing a variety of past program decisions (get your non-HR colleagues to help you to track them), you need to identify the critical success factors in getting each individual to vote yes. For each influential individual, you must identify their primary decision "mindset." Individuals make decisions in a variety of ways, but they generally fall under these "mindset" categories: financial, logical, scientific, emotional, image, personal relationships, selfish, or immediacy of impact. Identify the minimum acceptable number or "passing score" you need to reach for each of the criteria (for example: 11% is the minimum acceptable ROI percentage).

- Determine who is likely to resist or support it, and why. Identify which individuals routinely support or vote against HR or other "overhead" programs. Try to identify a "commonality" or a pattern in the decision-making in order to identify "why" they approve some but reject others.

2. Demonstrate that the individuals proposing this program are credible. It's unfortunate but true that mediocre programs supported and presented by great people get funded more often than great programs presented by mediocre people. In order to prove that you and your team are credible, you must make a strong case that you are "experts" in your industry, in your business, and in this topic area.

- Prove that you are an expert in the problems and opportunities of your industry and your firm. You can prove that you are an expert in forecasting the future problems and opportunities in your industry and at your firm. You can increase your credibility by citing examples of the business impact that your past programs have had. Show that you have done detailed research in your program area and that you can answer any question on the subject without hesitation.

- Forecast trends and patterns. Show that you know where the business and industry are going by highlighting key trends and patterns. Include forecasts for the changing business and environmental factors.

- Demonstrate your success rate and your track record. You must demonstrate that the previous programs and projects you have presented have reached their goals and had positive, measurable business impacts. Quantify the success rate of your past projects in percentages.

- Show that the HR "owner" of the project is well-known, trusted, and respected. Make sure that the person running the program is known and respected by the decision-makers. Improve your case by providing information to show that they have the experience, track record, and expertise necessary to run a successful program. Determine whether the program sponsor has any major enemies or major program failures in their background. If they are new to the firm, assume that they will encounter the NIH (not-invented-here) syndrome. Provide information to show that they "think like us."

3. Demonstrate that the program helps the firm meet its goals and that the program fits your culture.

All overhead programs come under scrutiny, because it's not always easy to show how they directly impact business results. However, executives still need to see the direct relationship between the proposed HR programs and the stated corporate goals and objectives for this year.

No matter how effective a program might appear on the surface, decision-makers often use a "cultural filter" to screen out programs that don't seem to fit their corporate culture or values. If you are unsure on this one, get a "grizzled veteran" to do a quick cultural fit assessment. Convincing executives that there is a cultural fit often means the judicial use of key buzzwords, citing historical precedents, and mentioning corporate heroes. Having a corporate "veteran" sponsor the program can also alleviate fears that it doesn't fit your corporate culture.

- Show that your solution helps meet your corporate business goals and objectives. Be sure to repeat the key objectives in your documentation and show how the solution directly aligns with the major ones. Quantify the estimated impacts.

- Clarify whether it fixes an existing problem or is a new opportunity. Most executives choose fixing existing problems over seeking out "new" profit opportunities. If you select a problem to fix, first identify the problem, and then show its causes and quantify the problem's impacts. Next, show how your solution solves the problem. Where possible, give examples of where this type of solution has solved this problem in other similar organizations. If it is an opportunity, demonstrate how the results will be superior to competing opportunities, and demonstrate that there is a sense of urgency that requires immediate action.

- Demonstrate how it fits your culture and your processes. Show how each other major program elements fits, supports, or enhances your culture and values. If the program has brought impacts, show how the solution aligns or at least does not conflict with your ongoing processes and systems.

- Show that it impacts on diversity. Where possible, quantify the impact the program will have on increasing the diversity of your workforce.

4. Demonstrate how it helps improve your firm's competitive position.
Executives and decision-makers are almost always competitive people. They love programs that give a sustainable competitive advantage over rival firms and their products. An HR program is most effective when it is the first and only one in the marketplace. Once everyone has one, they become essentially a commodity — which means that it's necessary to have one, but having one gives you no significant edge.

- Show how it gives you a competitive advantage. Demonstrate (and then quantify) how this program is superior to those of your competitors. Provide a side-by-side comparison of the program features of what they offer and what you offer.

- Demonstrate how it allows you to differentiate us. Show that the program is unique enough so that it will stand out among the rest. Show how that uniqueness will get us "talked about" in our industry. Describe the unique programming elements and demonstrate how they are difficult to copy.

- Show that it makes "us" just like them. Senior managers almost always have a "model" organization that they want to be like. Demonstrate how this program will make us more like Cisco or other benchmark organizations. Show what they do and how this program will emulate them.

- Demonstrate that you have done your benchmarking. Show that you've done your research and benchmarking by outlining the best practices at each of the leading firms.

- Forecast where your competitors "will be." If you assume that any program implementation will take some time, show that you have calculated how far the competitor will have advanced by the time your program is implemented — and what you have done to counter that progress.

- Forecast what response they will make to your program. Include in your program plan the steps you will take in order to combat their inevitable counter move or copying of our program.

5. Demonstrate that there is a high probability of success.

All programs involve risks, and "people programs" have some of the highest failure rates. It's essential that you demonstrate both in probabilities and in dollars the likelihood of success of your program. Be prepared to show how you arrived at the success rate.

- Prove how often these types of solutions work. Demonstrate that you've done your research, and quantify how often these types of programs work and fail.

- List the critical success/failure factors. If you can't show why a program succeeds, you are clearly not an expert. Show that you've done your research by listing and prioritizing the critical success factors for this type of program. Also, make a list of the common problems that can occur in implementing this type of program, and show that you have a solution for each.

- List the environmental and economic factors that impact the likelihood of success. Programs and solutions are impacted by changes in the internal and external environment. List the key environmental factors that impact program success. Show how you will monitor and track each of these.

- Demonstrate that you have the talent, technology, or other competencies necessary for success. Great ideas fail without the right resources. Demonstrate that we have the necessary talent to manage and operate the programming. Show that we have the necessary competencies and experience, and that we have the infrastructure or technology necessary for success.

6. Demonstrate the possible economic impacts.

Speaking the language of business means using dollars and numbers. HR professionals need to "talk" the language of business and finance if they expect to be listened to. Although every company has its own unique measures of business success, the following list is a good representation of most business success measures.

Don't get hung up on "perfect " numbers. Finance estimates such things as sales, profits, and goodwill all the time. However, be sure that you run your proposed project success measures and metrics by someone in the CFO's office before you formally present your program plan. Where possible, involve financial professionals in setting up the acceptable success measures. Beware of traditional internal HR success measures, because they are too tactical. Senior executives focus on overall business impacts. Incidentally, great hiring, retention, and people productivity programs generally have among the highest ROI of any business programs, so don't be shy with the numbers.

- Improve revenue, income, profit, margins, customer value, and shareholder value. Estimate the potential impact of the program on profits. Next, focus on shareholder value or stock price. Finally, can you demonstrate that through better hiring, training, pay practices, or technology, the firm will improve its productivity and profits?

- Calculate the payback period. Executives hate to wait a long time for the programming break-even point. Demonstrate how many months it will be before the program begins generating results, and when the initial investment will be paid back.

- Minimize the amount of up-front money needed. The "best" overhead programs operate out of existing resources. Hiring new people and buying equipment are red flag items. Executives want to minimize the amount of up-front money that is needed to get a program started. Try to show that results will be demonstrated before any additional cash is needed.

- List the program success measures (metrics). List the five key success measures for the program or project. Be sure to include the minimal "passing score" for each measure.

- Calculate the program's ROI. New programs or projects are frequently measured by their return on investment. Demonstrate that for every dollar invested, at least one dollar and 15 cents will be returned (a 15 percent ROI). ROIs of above 50 percent are not credible (outside of drug-dealing circles).

- Calculate its impact on our products and services. Anything that improves our product almost always impresses executives. Demonstrate, where you can, that the improved HR programs (hiring, training, etc.) will dramatically improve each of the following business impact measures:

  - Increased margins
  - Increased market share
  - Your time-to-market for product development
  - Added product features or product quality
  - Improved response time or customer service
  - Decreased errors or rejects
  - Decreased cycle or process time
  - Increased customer satisfaction
  - Increased image, PR, or brand recognition
  - Increased product sales (which might differ from increased profit)

- Show that your program facilitates your company's rapid growth. Modern executives love "top-line growth." Programs that facilitate or allow rapid growth almost always receive a high priority.

- Calculate its impact on products and services. Anything that improves your product almost always impresses executives. Demonstrate, where you can, that improved hiring and training will do so.

- Show the likelihood of external financial support. Programs that are partially funded by outside sources (strategic partners, the government, customers, or vendors) have an increased likelihood of support. This is because you have already demonstrated that others also see value in what you're doing, and they're willing to vote with their wallets.

7. Demonstrate that your project plan is credible.
Great programs are often not approved because their implementation plans are weak. Generally, project plans are not judged as credible because they fail to answer key questions or they fail to anticipate potential problems. Have your plan reviewed by a successful internal project manager and, over time, develop a checklist for assessing program implementation plans.

- Show that the project lead is credible. If you have to "sell" the individual to the management team, you are already in trouble. Pick someone they know and trust.

- Demonstrate that your team is competent. Provide a brief profile of each team member, highlighting their skills and demonstrating their accomplishments in recent projects or programs. Delete any team members who might have a "negative" image.

- Show that you can attract any talent we might need. If it is a new program, you must demonstrate that you will be able to learn quickly or attract experienced talent either internally or from the outside.

- List the program steps. Don't skimp here. Provide an appendix document that lists in some detail each of the steps you will take to implement the program. The goal here is to demonstrate that you have thought of all eventualities and that you have a logical step-by-step process.

- Show that you have undertaken a pilot. Executives say that they are risk-takers, but in fact they are really "calculated" risk-takers. By proposing or actually operating a pilot project or beta test, you can demonstrate that you are willing to try out and refine your idea before any "big dollars" are required. If you have already done a successful pilot by using your own resources, you're halfway there.

- Highlight the program monitoring system. Great implementation plans include "milestones" or assessment points where the program is re-evaluated. Sometimes weak programs are approved when they demonstrate that they have an effective feedback loops that allows them to continually improve and learn.

- Provide best-/worst-case scenarios. Executives live in a reality where things often go wrong. Effective project plans anticipate things going wrong, so they highlight every possible eventuality. Demonstrate that you have considered both best- and worst-case scenarios — that you have calculated their probabilities and have a backup plan for each.

- Show a plan for identifying any "unintended consequences." Even great programs can have side effects. Demonstrate that you have a formal program that is designed to identify any potential negative or positive "unintended consequences" that might occur as an indirect result of your program.

- Identify any potential legal issues. Executives often hate lawyers, but they hate surprises even more. Show that you have calculated any legal risks and taken them into account.

8. Make sure that individuals perceive that the program offers them some direct personal benefits.

Executives can be prone to selfishness — after all, getting to the top generally requires some degree of it. Don't ignore that fact. Treat them as individuals with egos, insecurities, and feelings. Make sure that you demonstrate to each of the influential ones how the program will benefit them personally. In reverse, you also need to look at how the program might threaten them or their business unit. Ignore this element of the business case at your peril!

- Establish a personal relationship with the decision-maker. On more than one occasion, great programs have been rejected because the program manager failed to build a personal relationship with the influential decision-makers. Remember, it is easier to reject strangers than it is friends. Make sure that they are aware of any common interests or experiences you might share.

- Demonstrate that the program improves "my" chance of promotion or increased income. Where possible, demonstrate to each individual decision-maker how the program might help their career or boost their income level.

- Demonstrate that the program might build "my" image. Executives can have enormous egos, so be sure to demonstrate how the project might improve their visibility and image both inside and outside the corporation.

9. Be ready to:
- Be offered a reduced budget. Be prepared for the eventuality that they will approve your project but at a reduced budget level. Anticipate this eventuality, and have a backup plan that allows you to operate at partial funding. Be prepared, however, to say "No, thanks," if partial funding will doom you to failure.

- Include a continuous improvement process in your plan. Include in your plan a process for continually upgrading and improving every key element of your program. This program element will excite even the most mundane decision-maker.

- Take into account people's past experiences with your department. Many executives have had negative experiences with the HR Department. Don't be naive. Study the history, and be prepared to show how you are different or have changed.

10. If all else fails ...

- Be aware that executives are almost always a macho group. Whether they are men or women, they are universally impressed with people who stick their necks out, because they themselves must stick their necks out every day. They are also painfully aware that most "overhead" people (and HR is no different) are risk-adverse. If you really want the project to be approved, you need to "draw a line in the sand" and put your job on the line. This means:

    - Guarantee the date the program will be operational
    - Set that date to be within 90 days
    - Guarantee numerical results (specify them) within six months of operation
    - Guarantee further numerical results at the end of the year
    - And finally ... offer to resign if the above four don't occur!

- Any questions?

The Service-Level Agreement:
A Tool for True Professionals Who Deliver

It is a commonly held view that among all overhead functions found in corporations, HR has one of the poorest reputations. Yet that reputation is something many in HR attempt to do nothing about (other than complain).

Because I spend a great amount of time with corporate managers and HR professionals, I get to hear both sides as to why this is. As it turns out, managers are disappointed with what HR delivers, and HR is often disappointed with how managers manage.

One of the many reasons for these disappointments is that the relationship between the two parties is never clearly defined. A second reason for the conflict is that the power relationship between the two parties is unequal. In this case, the managers seem to have all of the power. The third reason is that there are few metrics to ensure that the work is getting done at Six Sigma quality and on time.

An excellent way to improve this relationship is to clearly define the rights, expectations, and roles of each party in a service-level agreement.

What Is an SLA (Service-Level Agreement)?

An SLA is just that: an agreement to provide a certain defined "level" (variable with the price) of delivered service. An SLA has three basic parts:

1. It is a formal written agreement to provide a certain level of "measurable service" to a customer.

2. It defines the effort level that the manager must provide in order to complete the tasks that are "owned" in the process.

3. It describes performance metrics and related rewards.

Service-level agreements are widely used in many customer service functions, and often with external vendors, but rarely have they been used to define the relationship between one function of an organization and another.

HP was a pioneer in offering service-level agreements in HR. Starting in the 1990s, managers were given the opportunity to choose between several different levels of HR service, from the "Cadillac level" to the "VW bug" level. Managers could pay less in overhead if they needed fewer services. In fact, managers with fewer employee relations problems and turnover issues actually needed less HR help because they did a great job as managers. Why not reward managers (by cutting their costs) for being effective people managers?

Sun Micro went even further in providing "choices." Its fee-for-service approach allowed some managers to choose to utilize no internal HR services at all in some areas, and even to go outside for the HR services they wanted.

HR Professionals Can't Spell Customer Service?

How is HR at providing customer service to employees, applicants, and managers? Ask a customer service expert to rate your HR processes, and their response will be almost universal: the worst customer service outside of a prison (or DMV)! Service-level agreements can change all of that because:

1. They initially spell out roles and expectations.

2. Their heavy measurement and reward components incent all to do their part.

Benefits of an SLA

A service-level agreement is a formal contract in which the roles and responsibilities of the managers and the recruiters are spelled out. For each deliverable, there is a metric that looks at performance in terms of time, quality, volume, cost, and satisfaction level. These metrics, coupled with rewards, ensure that all parties to the agreement do their part.

Customers have responsibilities, too! Managers, employees, and — yes — even applicants are customers of HR services. These customers have a shared responsibility to do their part or face the consequences. Service-level agreements require managers to be responsive when they are called upon to do something that requires their ownership or participation. Managers are traditionally unwilling to commit much time or effort to HR tasks, because they often see few immediate benefits in it. They also see HR as being unresponsive. Service agreements can help even the playing field because they look at both the performance of HR as well as the actions (or lack of action) of the hiring managers.

Incidentally, service-level agreements are just one part of a growing trend to make HR act less like a bureaucracy and more like a competitive business that is responsive to customer needs.

The next step you can expect to see in HR is the "fee-for-service model," as alluded to above. In this model, managers pay only for the individual HR services that they actually use. This means that managers who do a great job of retention, recruiting, and motivating employees (and therefore need little help) don't have to use any level of HR service. They in essence get to buy as little HR as they want. In contrast, a manager who needs a lot of employee relations and training help will have to pay for it.

What Does a Service-Level Agreement Look Like?
A Service-Level Agreement has three basic parts:

Part I — Deliverables
The first element of the agreement is a listing of the services and tasks that the manager requires. In recruiting, for example, the "deliverables" could be sourcing, requisition help, screening, or even offer letters. For each task or "deliverable," there would be a defined level-of-service metric in as many as five areas:

- Quality

- Costs (a range of costs)

- Time (a minimum and maximum response time and delivery dates)

- Quantity (the minimum and maximum volume or quantity level)

- Satisfaction (a minimum level of customer satisfaction)

Part II — Rewards and Penalties

For each task and defined level of service, there would be a defined cost. In addition, there might be a reward for exceeding any of the five service-level metrics. There might also be a penalty for not meeting the goals.

Part III — Responsibilities of the "Customer"

This is the part that makes HR happy. The manager would be required to carry out responsibilities as well. Using recruitment services as an example, under the agreement, a manager would be responsible for fulfilling a certain number of recruiting tasks. These responsibilities might include:

- Filling out requisitions and job descriptions accurately

- Reading resumes within a certain period of time

- Completing interviews within a certain period of time

- Selecting the finalists within a certain time

- Making a certain number of reference calls

- Ensuring that interviewers are trained in interviewing and the law

- Completing the offer process within a specified period

- Completing documentation within the specified time

- Completing an effective orientation process

- Responding to questions from recruiters within a reasonable period

HR is then responsible for maintaining the metrics and reporting the results. Managers who meet their deliverables would be rewarded with a higher level of priority (in response time) and with lower costs. Managers who fail to meet their goals would be served with a lower priority and, in some cases, services would be withheld from a manager as a consequence of failing to meet responsibilities. Performance metrics would be reported to top management so that they can judge both the effectiveness of HR and the extent to which individual managers are helping or hindering HR efforts.

This chapter highlighted two important but under-utilized tools that are available to HR managers. Most require the extensive use of "promises" that are backed up by numbers. Although both require some degree of preparation, following the outline can have many positive results. Not only do they both produce dramatic results, but also, even more importantly, they force HR professionals to think like businesspeople. But isn't that what HR metrics are all about? They mean:

- Forcing HR professionals to become fact-based rather than opinion-based

- Requiring HR programs to measure themselves the same way that P&L business units are measured

- Encouraging HR professionals to make promises about service delivery just the way business units must guarantee service levels to the firm's customers

What does this all mean? It means that "avoiding metrics" within HR is no longer a viable option. It's time to step back and re-examine HR. After over a decade of calling ourselves "business partners," in reality, we have failed to live up to the name. Both my professional HR and academic experience have led me to a singular focus on metrics. Why? Because I have found that, without exception, the very best HR departments and the top HR professionals already "live and die in the numbers." Isn't it time that you did, too?

Chapter Nine

Building Your Personal Action Plan

9

Up until now, this book has talked about why metrics are needed, how you can assess each function, and how to make data collected more consistent. If you are like many, you're probably wondering where to start once you are convinced that metrics are needed.

Many people scratch their heads when attempting to figure this point out, so I have developed a few questions that, when answered, should leave you with a pretty clear picture of what needs to be done.

Eight Questions You Need to Answer

1. What deliverables are most critical to your organization's success?
This question suggests that you look outside your role or function, and identify the firm's critical deliverables in the coming months and years. (Unfortunately for most organizations, this is not a stable list, and it will change dramatically as the organization progresses through its life cycle.) Once you know what the business must deliver (products, processes, or services), you can then create a starting ground on which to identify what functional initiatives and programs you can provide in order to facilitate the organization's meeting its own critical deliverables.

2. What are your business unit's major deliverables?
Having identified what is critical to the organization, you now turn your attention from the overall firm perspective to the local level by identifying

what your local business unit's major deliverables are. To a large degree, each of these deliverables from the business unit should map to (or mesh with) those of the larger organization.

3. What are potential trouble spots?

Still, before you move forward with solutions, you need to identify which deliverables have caused the most problems (pain points) in the past. By identifying past issues, you can better prepare for them. You can also forecast areas where you may experience difficulties in the near future. You need to eventually develop a metric for each potential trouble spot.

4. Who are your key customers?

This question is asking you to identify which deliverables (products and services) belong to each unit, and, more importantly, the customer or owner of each.

5. What are the customer's expectations and how can success be measured?

Now it's time to turn your attention toward identifying the customer's expectations. What are the objective characteristics that will define the success of the product or service in the customer's eyes? When evaluating the customer's expectations, be sure to keep in mind what primary and secondary measures (metrics) might be appropriate in order to assess whether the customer's current and future expectations are being met. Follow up with a breakdown of the potential metrics, and force the customer to rank them by importance.

6. What specific problems have you forecasted?

This question, along with the two that follow, start to bring your attention down to the specific metrics that will serve as your diagnostic dashboard. To answer this question, hone in on where current products or services are failing to meet customer expectations. Then, attempt to ascertain *why* each of the products or services is not reaching the bar. The answers to this question will indicate what aspects of performance need to be measured on an ongoing diagnostic basis, so that the impact of the changes can be seen.

7. What external pressures might adversely impact success?

External pressures and environmental changes can impact product and program success. Good areas to look at (for the presence of external pressures) are demographics, economic factors, and competitor actions. Forecast how are they changing, and the impact of these changes on the potential success of your critical deliverables.

8. What are performance points associated with each deliverable (product or service)?

The goal is simple: To establish a baseline that future measurements can be evaluated against. A baseline point allows you to assess change, whether positive or negative.

9. Have you identified where and how to gather the data necessary for each performance metric?

Check with managers and IT about the availability and the quality of the data you need. Run a test to verify.

10. Have you gotten management buy-in on your metrics?

Before implementing your final set of metrics pre-test them on senior financial, IT, and management professionals. If possible, run a "pilot" to refine them. Implement and revise over time.

HR Metrics and You

I hope that you have enjoyed this journey through the world of HR metrics as much as you will eventually benefit from it. As we know, HR can be a powerful force behind business success, and hopefully this book can now be a powerful force behind your own HR effort.

If you are a Human Resources professional, building the business case for HR can now become a reality.

If you are a CEO, CFO, or COO, you should now have a better understanding of what metrics you should demand from your HR team.

If you are a student or neophyte in HR, I hope that you have now seen the future of your profession. In addition, I hope that you are inspired to become part of a profession where it is common knowledge that good, profitable business derives from good, *provable* HR.

I have full confidence in your increased success.

Appendix

Additional Sources of Information

Answerthink, Inc. (a/k/a The Hackett Group)
1001 Brickell Bay Drive, Ste. 3000
Miami, FL 33131
305-375-8005
www.answerthink.com

Hackett Benchmarking & Research has been a leading provider of information on HR best practices since 1988. Each year, they publish numerous reports on the efficiency and effectiveness of various business functions at more than 1,600 global companies.

The Employment Management Association
1800 Duke Street
Alexandria, VA 22314
703-548-3440
www.shrm.org/ema

The Employment Management Association was acquired in 1998 as the employment arm of the larger Society for Human Resource Management. It offers in-depth information on all aspects of employment and retention, including periodic surveys of widely accepted staffing metrics.

International Personnel Management Association (IPMA)
1617 Duke Street
Alexandria, VA 22314
703-549-7100
www.ipma-hr.org

The IPMA is a nonprofit, membership-funded organization founded to promote excellence within the Human Resources function. In striving to reach this goal, they annually produce benchmark reports covering Compensation, Recruitment, Selection, and Training.

The Saratoga Institute
3600 Pruneridge Avenue, Suite 380
Santa Clara, CA 95051
408-556-1150
www.saratoga-institute.com

The Saratoga Institute is the world's leading provider of benchmark best practices data for Human Resources. Each year, it publishes the Human Capital Benchmarking Report, which is filled with data collected from hundreds of organizations across more than 20 industries.

Staffing.org
P.O. Box 551
Plymouth Meeting, PA 19462
610-292-8561
www.staffing.org

Staffing.org, which is associated with Bernard Hodes, is a Web-based non-profit organization that is focused on the collection and dissemination of staffing-related metrics data. The annual report produced by Staffing.org has been reviewed by over 500 top HR and recruiting professionals.

Zigon Performance Group
604 Crum Creek Road
Media, PA 19063
610-891-9599
www.zigonperf.com

Zigon Performance Group (ZPG) is a management consulting firm specializing in all phases of performance management. They create custom systems for performance appraisal, performance management, and team performance measurement. The ZPG Web site includes the QuickMeasures Idea Database, which provides possible individual performance measures for over 429 job families.